On Cyberwarfare

"The beginning of all things are small."

--Cicero

Acknowledgements

This book was an enjoyable undertaking and I am almost sad to finish it. My main aim was attempting to distill as much knowledge and experience as possible regarding cyberwar for the lay or even experienced reader as possible. I hope perhaps it will be as intriguing to read as it was fun for me to write.

More importantly, I could not have done it alone. My heartfelt thanks go out to LCDR Marzetta (USN) and Derick Fan for our discussion on economics, Jim for our talks on his ideas regarding innovation/industrial security and finally those involved in the intelligence field and special warfare who offered their own insights along the way.

And last but not least, Ying-Ying Lu and my family who stood by me the whole time, offering continual encouragement when it felt like I would never finish. Thank you.

Note: The views expressed are those of the author and do not reflect the official policy or position of the Department of Defense or the U.S. Government.

Preface

While considering the various aspects of available literature on cyberwarfare, I've noticed what appears to be a knowledge gap hobbling writers on the subject. Both popular and academic literature vacillates between either authors who possess a significant computer background but seem to struggle portraying the strategic and tactical implications of the views in a simplistic manner or authors who have advanced, unrelated degrees in liberal arts yet lack either experience or credentials in computing or related technology fields. In this book I hope to bridge that gap between the two disciplines, drawing on over a decade of experience with computers and communications in the military, ideas and experience in computers and communications both inside the military and out along with knowledge gained from my own personal studies in political science.[1]

The aim of this book will be to provide a basic foundation for cyberwar operations from both the strategic and tactical sense, spark new ideas for

---

[1]And coffee. Lots of coffee.

others in the government or military to bring about lasting change that will define our future and provide an accessible means of gaining knowledge on the rising tide of technological warfare for the reader who does not necessarily have the time to watch news on the progress of technology every day. This book also assumes that the reader is able to at a minimum use a Google search if the need arises to gain further understanding on certain types of software listed or to follow up on news stories.

Though forms of technological warfare have existed for decades, a renaissance is taking place in a modern day evolution towards cyberwarfare in the 21st century. The types and level of attacks have varied, ranging from the simplistic such as website defacements and crude jamming of radar systems to the impressively complex, such as sophisticated hacking attacks against critical infrastructure systems, drone mounted lasers and the creation of advanced malware (Malicious Software) such as Flame and Stuxnet.

As of recent days, talk regarding hacking and cyberwar around the world has grown more sharply focused as the threat becomes prevalent, however there appears to be a missing puzzle piece: The creation and development of a coherent Cyberwarfare (CW) doctrine. Responses to the sudden shock of CW tend to shift between seeking help from persons with little to no legitimate computer skills to occasionally throwing large amounts of money at the problem or even worse, doing nothing at all.

As humanity grows dependent on global technology, it is becoming more evident that we must develop a cogent framework of strategy and tactics of which a country should build on to protect itself. In this regard I will be attempting to further create a basic foundation of and detailing such a framework, including attempting to better elaborate on what exactly cyberwarfare is, advocating the creation of an enduring civilian-based cyberwarfare command, discussing the applicability of cyberwarfare in terminology similar to existing forms of warfare while offering suggestions for a new structure and method of pursuing attacks utilizing technology. Finally, we will look towards present day threats and take a view at what the future may hold down the road.

The popular conception of what cyberwar tends to be described solely in terms of computer based attacks via the Internet. This prevailing stereotype was mostly created and continues to be reinforced through popular movies, literature and major news outlets among means. Though partially correct, this definition is not expansive enough. I believe a more dramatically expanded definition is necessary, namely the following: Cyberwarfare is the use or exploitation of technology by an individual, group or nation to aid in the accomplishment of their political goals. Exploiting technology goes far beyond systems connected to the Internet, and can include independent technological systems such as cell phones, cars, industrial control systems, GPS receivers/satellites, TV signals, satellites, computer based systems disconnected from the net or virtually any technology in existence that can be accessed in any fashion. Those involved with computer security are fond of the informal understanding, "Nothing is ever completely secure. It's just a matter of time." When we remove the shackles of misconception that chain cyberwarfare to a minimalist view which remains solely related to computers and the Internet, the expansive nature of this type of warfighting becomes comforting and worrying at the same time. It is comforting because we know what to look at and engage in but also worrying because others are also able to accomplish the same through similar means.

With a brief description of what the desired aims for this book is and a definition of cyberwarfare in hand, we will now move forward, beginning with developing a vision of the present and future of cyberwarfare while laying fertile foundation for other ideas to spring forth.[2]

---

[2] Footnotes will be used for amplifying information on software while news citations are current as of writing. Credible web sources have been chosen to help the reader find supporting information more quickly.

Chapter 1: History of Cyberwarfare

Often, when looking at the different avenues in cyberwar there is typically derision from some corners regarding how effective this type of warfare can actually be. Some even go further, suggesting that no such type of warfare even exists. However the reality is that through the new definition of cyberwar as compared to a traditional definition, we can chart history in a different way, including anti-satellite weapons, electronic warfare and attempts to hack real time communications. This section will list some of the more prominent moments in the history of modern cyberwar so we can roughly gauge where the current state of affairs stands and disabuse the notion that it does not exist through real world, historical examples of successful attacks. These moments in history should be viewed through a clairvoyant lens as the future tends to reflect past thoughts and innovation. While peering through some of these accounts of prior history, what should be held close to mind is not the actual technology that was used but rather the innovative mentality which enabled the success of such actions.

The general approach towards turning the tide of computer based attacks usually involves an approach of using automated tools, using minimal and basic security protocols and other feeble attempts to protect systems. However this "fortify the castle" strategy will grow increasingly difficult both to implement and maintain as time progresses as those who are conducting the attacks will continue to grow more innovative and use guerilla style attacks to render such a defense moot. We will see this story repeated often while looking over attacks: A technology is created that is considered quite defensible, then an innovative individual comes along and stuns all present through managing to discover a chink in the armor that no one had ever considered. And this will continue to happen again and again until the emphasis is shifted from static defense to using active, continuous human transformation and innovation to help stem the tide of such an assault.

It is additionally worth noting that even in traditional warfare the same narrative is played out time and again as far back as the Roman military attempting to defeat the Gaul's, the American revolutionary insurrection against the British and Mao Zedong's fight against the Chinese government. Either those in control of corporations or holding the reins of power in government can address the problem more effectively or history books in the future will address the failure of doing so.

A rich historical tapestry exists involving attacks via the electromagnetic spectrum and other technological means, however attempting to cover such a topic in depth would fill up entire volumes. There are many notable attacks that have occurred in recent years, however for brevity purposes the following examples will instead focus more on recent computer based attacks. Below are a few examples of significant, more modern, technological and computer based attacks that show how far we have come in terms of technology and the resultant continuing vulnerability of computer systems around the world.

Country Attacks

2013 October- North Korea conducted multiple Distributed Denial of Service (DDOS) attacks throughout the year against South Korean targets, costing the government an estimated $800 million dollars. Earlier in the year, South Korea was also the recipient of multiple computer based attacks attributed to North Korea which wiped out a significant amount, if not all data on almost 30,000 PC's with banks and TV stations among their targets. [3]

2013 September- British signals intelligence agency GCHQ was discovered to be conducting complex operations to gain access into major Belgian telecommunications corporation Belgacom. (Codename: Operation Socialist) This attack used a variety of methods to attempt and gain access to the corporation's core GRX routers, including through identifying key staff to target and man in the middle attacks. (MITM) Telecommunication giants core GRX routers are used to carry international traffic and would have provided excellent intelligence to be exploited. [4]

2012 September- Chinese government hackers were able to breach the White House military network through a spear phishing attack, providing the

---

[3] Arthur, Charles. "North Korea behind Hacking Attack in March, Claims Seoul." *Guardian Weekly*. Guardian News and Media, 10 Apr. 2013. Web. 04 Feb. 2014.

[4] "British Spy Agency GCHQ Hacked Belgian Telecoms Firm." *Spiegel Online International*. N.p., 20 Sept. 2013. Web. 04 Feb. 2014.

attackers access to an unclassified portion of their network. [5]

2010 September- The United States (though some sources speculate Israeli involvement.) utilized what has been termed the most complex malware ever seen (Codename: Stuxnet) to attack and cause the destruction of at least 1,000 centrifuges at the Nantanz nuclear enrichment facility in Iran. With a meager size of 500kb, it was a specially crafted piece of offensive computer software that sought out Siemens industrial control computers inside the Nantanz facility used to control and then destroy their nuclear centrifuges. Stuxnet was able to use a novel method of infecting industrial supervisory control and data acquisition (SCADA) systems so as to alter the speed at which the centrifuges moved, speeding them up for a set period of time and slowing them down which eventually resulted in their destruction. There are differing accounts as to how much damage was truly suffered, however the idea to attack the

---

[5] McCullagh, Declan. "White House Confirms 'spearphishing' Intrusion." *CNET News*. CBS Interactive, 01 Oct. 2012. Web. 04 Feb. 2014.

computer systems of industrial equipment to cause physical damage was one of the first of its kind. [6]

2008- The United States Department of Defense suffered a serious compromise in its Central Command networks by the Agent.btz malware. The malware was introduced via a USB stick left at a base in the Middle East which contained software that created backdoors for remote command and control software. The remote command and control software provided the ability for outside attackers to gain control of the system and took the DOD over a year to remove. The fallout of this malware became part of the impetuous for the beginning for the US militaries first cyber command. [7]

2007- The Chinese government was accused of hacking into US Military NIPRNET systems. Though the system only carries unclassified information and does not represent the level of the SIRPNET (which carries classified information), however the attacks displayed the ability for modern day military systems

---

[6] Kushner, David. "The Real Story of Stuxnet." *IEEE Spectrum*. N.p., 26 Feb. 2013. Web. 17 Feb. 2014.
[7] Zetter, Kim. "The Return of the Worm That Ate the Pentagon." *Wired.com*. Conde Nast Digital, 07 Dec. 0011. Web. 17 Feb. 2014.

to be penetrated via computer means and acted as a black eye for the US Military.[8] The Chinese government, as it typical does, denied involvement in any way saying that such attacks were illegal and that they would deal with such issues in accordance with the law.

2006 August- Spear phishing attacks were conducted by the Chinese government against targets around the world, including the US, Canadian and Taiwanese governments. (Codename: Operation Shady RAT) Other targets included Computer Security companies, Defense contractors, the Department of Energy and various other international political targets. (Including the United Nations, the International Olympic Committee and the World Anti-Doping agency.) When users clicked on the link provided in an email, a command and control server would be downloaded which would then open up the floodgates for outside malicious users to login in and conduct further attacks/attempt to steal information. [9]

---

[8] Marqu, Robert. "China Emerges as Leader in Cyberwarfare." *The Christian Science Monitor*. N.p., 14 Sept. 2007. Web. 17 Feb. 2014.
[9] Lau, Hon. "The Truth Behind the Shady RAT." *Endpoint, Cloud, Mobile & Virtual Security Solutions*. N.p., 23 Jan. 2014. Web. 17 Feb. 2014.

Corporate Attacks

2013 October- Adobe suffered a major cyberattack, compromising up to 150 million customers information, including user names, passwords, credit card and debit card numbers, expiration dates and other information relating to customer orders.[10]

2012 August- The largest oil company in Saudi Arabia, ARAMCO was attacked by a previously unknown hacking group calling itself the Cutting Sword of Justice via the Shamoon virus. The attack temporarily took over and destroyed data on 75% of ARAMACO's computers, effectively placing them offline. [11]

2012 August- Two weeks after the ARAMCO incident, Qatari based RAS Gas, a major natural gas exporter was hit by the Shamoon malware as well making the company website and e-mail servers unavailable for multiple days. [12]

2012 February- Taiwan semi-conductor company FoxConn was hacked by a group calling itself Swagg

---

[10] Frank, Blair. "Adobe Breach Hit More than 150 Million Usernames and Passwords." *GeekWire*. N.p., 11 July 2013. Web. 17 Feb. 2014.

[11] Perlroth, Nicole. "In Cyberattack on Saudi Firm, U.S. Sees Iran Firing Back." *NY Times*. N.p., 23 Oct. 2012. Web. 17 Feb. 2014.

[12] Mills, Elinor. "Virus Knocks out Computers at Qatari Gas Firm RasGas." *CNET News*. CBS Interactive, 30 Aug. 2012. Web. 17 Feb. 2014.

Security in retaliation for alleged terrible working conditions of mainland Chinese workers. After the hack, Swagg posted employee logins of the entire company on the Internet. [13]

2011 July- Internet Service Provider SK Communications, a subsidiary of South Korean based SK Telecom Co. Ltd was hacked via a malicious Trojan software update giving access to information on over 35 million accounts. [14]

2009- Software company Google was struck with a complex hack (Codename: Operation Aurora) by Chinese cyberunit PLA 6139. (aka the People's Liberation Army Advanced Persistent Threat Unit.) This penetration involved attempting to surreptitiously steal source code while also attempting to glean information on different corporations and the Gmail accounts of Chinese dissidents such as Ai Wei Wei. Multiple other corporations later publicly confirmed that they were also targeted, include Northrop Grumman, Morgan Stanley, Dow Chemical Adobe

---

[13] Whitney, Lance. "Apple Supplier Foxconn Hit by Hackers." *CNET News*. CBS Interactive, 09 Feb. 2012. Web. 17 Feb. 2014.
[14] "SK Hack by an Advanced Persistent Threat." *Command Five*. N.p., Sept. 2011. Web. 17 Feb. 2014.

Systems, Juniper Networks, and Yahoo. Due to increasing pressure from the Chinese government to censor much (if not all) of its content along with this seeming blatant hacking attempt that was supported by the Chinese government, Google instead opted to move its operations out of China in response.[15]

Notable Attacks

2013 September- Israel was hit with an infrastructure attack by an unknown, yet seeming simplistic malware. The target of the attacks appeared to be the Carmel tunnel camera systems via Trojan horse, with sudden results. (Though there remains speculation that the tunnel systems were actually affected by a random, untargeted virus.) The malfunction that resulted from this virus caused significant problems for over two days, resulting in an immediate 20-minute lockdown during morning rush hour and forcing the tunnel to remain completely shut for 8

---

[15] Zetter, Kim. "Google Hack Attack Was Ultra Sophisticated, New Details Show." *Wired*. Conde Nast Digital, 12 Jan. 0010. Web. 17 Feb. 2014.

hours causing massive traffic congestion in one of the largest cities in Israel. [16]

2013 May- Hackers perpetuated a massive online theft of nearly 45 million dollars from the National Bank of Ras Al-Khaimah, based in the United Arab Emirates and Bank Muscat, based out of Oman. The theft involved breaking into bank databases, eliminating the withdrawal limits on certain pre-paid debit cards with magnetic strips and creating access codes for the cards. Mules in various countries, including the United States were then given access to the cards to which they went on a withdrawal frenzy, looting over 45 million dollars from 27 countries in only 10 hours. 20% of the money stolen was kept by the thieves, with the rest being laundered through gifting luxury items back to varying countries back to the original hackers. The New York cell of the group was rounded up, while the overseas perpetuators remain at large. Later one of the Middle Eastern banks, Bank Muscat disclosed it would be taking a $39 million dollar loss in part because of this

---

[16] "Cyber-terrorism Shut Down Israel's Carmel Tunnel." *Infosecurity*. N.p., 28 Oct. 2013. Web. 17 Feb. 2014.

operation, which was more than half of its first quarter earnings in 2013. [17]

2013 February- Chinese military hacking group APT1 successfully gained access to what appeared to be a US based municipal water filtration facility. Unbeknownst to the attackers, the "water filtration facility" was actually a cloud-based honeypot (A disguised trap intended for gathering information on hacking tactics) created by security researcher Kyle Wilhoit which provided significant information on the tactics used to break inside the system. [18]

2012 April- Hackers managed to penetrate credit card processing intermediary company Global Payments. Up to 10 million credit cards, including assorted Visa and Mastercard's were possibly compromised with Global Payment suffering a 9% stock drop soon after. [19]

---

[17] Santora, Marc. "In Hours, Thieves Took $45 Million in A.T.M. Scheme." *New York Times*. N.p., 09 Mar. 2013. Web. 17 Feb. 2014.
[18] Simonite, Tom. "Chinese Hacking Team Caught Taking Over Decoy Water Plant." *MIT Technology Review*. N.p., 02 Aug. 2013. Web. 17 Feb. 2014.
[19] Siddel, Robin, and Andrew Johnson. "Data Breach Sparks Worry." *The Wall Street Journal*. Dow Jones & Company, 30 Mar. 2012. Web. 17 Feb. 2014.

2012- The Persian service area of the British Broadcasting Corporation suffered a sophisticated cyber-attack which then director-general Mark Thompson inferred was perpetrated by Iran. The attack not only targeted BBC offices, but also attempted to jam BBC satellite feeds and denial of serviced London phone lines through automated robocalls.[20]

2008 November- Complex malware, (Codename: Conflicker) was detected. Conflicker is a computer virus that was able to infect up to 10 million computers around the world. The virus was able to infect virtually any Microsoft operating system of the time (Including Windows 2000, XP, Vista, Server 2003 and Server 2008) and rapidly propagate through a variety of means (Internet, Removable Media and Network shares) to turn computers into zombies, thus making them available for botnet activity. (Botnet's are groups of computers utilized for near anonymous DDOS attacks.) Fears over the virus were great enough that a so-called "Conflicker Cabal" was created, composed of organizations such as

---

[20] "BBC Suffers Cyber-attack following Iran Campaign." *Reuters*. Thomson Reuters, 12 Mar. 2013. Web. 17 Feb. 2014.

Microsoft, Symantec, ICANN, and Verisign to attempt and stymie its progress/remove it.

Damage was considerable, including against the French Navy (network infections forcing aircraft at several airbases to be grounded), the UK Ministry of Defense (Infecting Royal Navy warships, submarines and hospitals), and even forcing a temporary disconnection of the Police National computer in Manchester, hampering the ability of local police to conduct routine checks on people and vehicles.[21]

2008 January- A massive protest movement, Operation Chanology began under the auspices of loosely organized hacktivist group Anonymous against the Church of Scientology. After the church successfully used legal takedown threats to remove what it perceived to be an unflattering video from Youtube, an infuriated Anonymous (who generally espouses the free flow of information across the Internet) retaliated both via cyber based means (Black faxing, website DDoS, hacking etc.), and also through worldwide protests which brought considerable

---

[21] O'Brien, Terrence. "What Is the Conficker Virus and Should You Be Worried?" *Switched*. N.p., 28 Jan. 2009. Web. 17 Feb. 2014.

negative attention towards the church. Legal efforts were also made against the church, including attempting to have their tax exempt status revoked. [22]

2008 August- A laptop on the International Space Station was infected with the w32.Gammima.AG worm. Speculation indicated that the worm, a low level threat, either infected the initial software load of the laptop or that a member who came aboard the station had accidently infected laptops through a removable disk. This adverse event is generally only significant in the sense that the worm was on the ISS, however the take away should be that even if completely isolated from the Internet and in space, a system network can still be infected. [23]

2007 April- Estonia was hit with an ongoing, nearly 1 million computer strong DDOS attack which swamped websites that were a part of multiple Estonian organizations, including parliament, banks, ministries and broadcasters. Reports also came in that Estonian

---

[22] Dibbell, Julian. "The Assclown Offensive: How to Enrage the Church of Scientology." *Wired*. Conde Nast Digital, 21 Sept. 2009. Web. 17 Feb. 2014.
[23] Gilbert, David. "International Space Station Infected With USB Stick Malware Carried on Board by Russian Astronauts." *International Business Times RSS*. N.p., 11 Nov. 2013. Web. 17 Feb. 2014.

emergency services number and fire service numbers were taken offline. Attacks were largely attributed to the Russian government, however further news reports seem to indicate that it was likely Russian hackers which the government either sanctioned or minimally at least condoned.[24]

Weapons buildup

2013 September- A British GCHQ program (Codename: EDGEHILL) for defeating encryption is discovered. EDGEHILL is a controversial program which was created for the purpose of decrypting commonly used encryption protocols for general Internet communications so as to more effectively spy on foreign entities.

2011 June- DARPA (Defense Advanced Research Projects Agency) announced plans to build the National Cyber Range. Plans are currently for a scale model of the Internet to be built so as to begin cyberwar game simulations with an eye towards advancing tactics and strategy.

---

[24] Davis, Joshua. "Hackers Take Down the Most Wired Country in Europe." *Wired.com*. Conde Nast Digital, 21 Aug. 2007. Web. 17 Feb. 2014.

Surveillance Programs

2013 June- GCHQ program (Codename: TEMPORA) was discovered. TEMPORA attempts to tap communications traffic on fiber optic lines between switching stations. It attempts to intercept as much information as possible based on pre-determined criteria to be put aside for further review. (Similar to the NSA's "ECHELON" program.)

2013- US Law enforcement program (Codename: Stingray) was discovered. The Stingray program was created and used in secrecy by the Federal Bureau of Investigation as a type of cellular tapping and triangulation system which utilized the creation of fake cell phone towers. This system allowed for the triangulation of cellular phones through radio based-GPS technology and also tapping virtually all information going to and from a phone, including text messages, phone calls and numbers called/incoming call numbers. The program was vigorously challenged after discovery due the fact that other members of the public could also inadvertently connect to the fake cellphone tower and thus give law enforcement information far beyond the scope of their warrant.

2010 June- Declassified NSA documents revealed the existence of the FIVE EYES program, an intelligence sharing agreement between intelligence organizations in several countries including the United States, Canada, Britain, New Zealand and Australia. The program has been criticized for possibly allowing spy agencies of various countries such as Britain and the United States to skillfully sidestep laws which were put in place to prevent them from spying on their citizens. For example, the British GCHQ could ask the American NSA to share information on British citizens with them, while the NSA could likewise request the GCHQ to provide information on American citizens thus both sides can essentially spy on their own citizens while publicly claiming they have not in actuality spied on the public.

Espionage

2012 June- Malware variant "Gauss" was discovered. Gauss is among the newer, complex cyber-weapons designed by nation-states for attack. Gauss was a worm created to infect user's computers in certain Lebanese banks, including the Bank of Beirut, FransaBank and Blombank with the intention of stealing a variety of sensitive personal information, including banking credentials. The malware acted covertly to gain general computer information, such as Network/Drive/BIOS information and browser passwords while also stealing login information for social networking accounts. Gauss is widely considered to be a relative of the malware variants Flame and Stuxunet and likely created by the same nation-state considering the surprising similarities in code. Following discovery, command and control servers for Gauss were deactivated in July 2012.

2011 October- American Predator and Reaper drones from Creech Air Force Base were discovered to have a persistent malware infection which possessed key logging capabilities. Multiple attempts were made to clear the rogue software to no avail, including full wipes of the hard drives themselves. It is currently believed that the software still lies on said systems due to an inability to remove the virus.[25]

2011 September- A new virus nicknamed Duqu was discovered by the Laboratory of Cryptography and

---

[25] Cluley, Graham. "Malware Compromises USAF Predator Drone Computer Systems." *Naked Security*. N.p., 10 Oct. 2011. Web. 17 Feb. 2014.

System Security at Budapest University. Operating in a very similar manner to Stuxnet, Duqu utilized keystroke loggers and other modules to steal sensitive information then smuggle said information out via JPEG picture files to command and control centers. The program was very similar to Stuxnet and seemed to almost exclusively target Iranian computers. After 36 days the virus was set to automatically self-destruct so as to help avoid detection. [26]

2010 May- Flame is one of the most advanced pieces of malware that has ever been discovered. Speculation has arisen as to whether the United States or Israel used this espionage tool to gain intelligence on multiple Middle Eastern countries, including Iran, Palestine, Sudan and Syria. This malicious software has the ability to gather data files, log keystrokes, turn on computer microphones to record conversations, take screen shots, copy instant messenger chats, etc. Of particular note is its ability to quickly propagate among multiple spectrums of

---

[26] "Duqu: A Stuxnet-like Malware Found in the Wild." *The Laboratory of Cryptography and System Security*. Budapest University of Technology and Economics, 14 Oct. 2011. Web. 17 Feb. 2014.

communications such as LAN and USB connections, activating the systems Bluetooth connection and finally transforming it into a beacon and sweeping the immediate area for other connections to siphon information.[27]

2009 December- Innovative thinking proved to be particularly shocking during the 2003 Iraqi War when it was discovered that Shiite militants were able to hack into American Predator and Reaper drone video feeds. At first brush this would lend credence to the possibility that insurgents had developed a stronger cyberwar capability, however the truth in these situations tends to be more mundane and boring. As the video feeds were discovered to be unencrypted, militants used laptops, a small satellite dish and simple $26 software named Skygrabber which can capture KU-Band and C-Band satellite feeds in the air and move it to a person's hard drive. During the latter days of the war, multiple insurgents were discovered to have entire drone video feeds on their laptops thanks to this simple, yet effective capture ability.

---

[27] "The Flame: Questions and Answers." *Securelist*. N.p., 28 May 2012. Web. 17 Feb. 2014.

2009 March- GhostNet was a massive international cyber-spying operation conducted by the People's Republic of China. Over 103 countries were hit, including the embassies of South Korea, Taiwan, Iran and Germany. The program was able to gain control over computers via emails with infected attachments, which would then provide access via command and control servers. Also of note was the occasional pushed download of the GhostRat utility, which would offer full, real-time access to the infected system, including giving the ability to turn on the local microphone, video camera and so forth. [28]

Considerations/Recommendations- Many of these attacks are within more recent years and reflect a snapshot of the current state of cyberwarfare. As can be seen based on a small snapshot of relatively recent events of which we are actually aware of or have been posted to the public, it is clear that not only has the age of cyberwarfare emerged but it has now reached the world as a defining tidal wave that we are already late in preparing for. In particular it is becoming more clear that the computer based side of

[28] Markoff, John. "Vast Spy System Loots Computers in 103 Countries." *New York Times*. N.p., 28 Mar. 2009. Web. 17 Feb. 2014.

technological warfare cannot be swept under the rug as "impotent" or "not really causing lasting damage." Perhaps it was a myth some time ago, however with the level of interconnectedness between systems and a considerable reliance on technology this is no longer the case.

Though perhaps for some countries the realization is late, we will however consider ways to both create enduring new agencies to deal with the threat and further improve upon modern CW through this book.

Chapter 2: Country Classifications

Creating a general classification of the technological sophistication of a country is an important starting point. Though technology pervades the globe, you see a range of technological ability ranging from the highly modernized (Korea, United States, Russia) to those which carry little more than basic radios or possibly not even electricity. Country classifications are a necessary starting part to begin ascertaining the effectiveness of levying cyberwar or if it is even financially feasible to utilize such measures. Through the system listed below, we will begin to develop a baseline and acquire a better awareness of how effective cyber capabilities can be applied while gaining a deeper understanding of other important points of possible weakness, such as the dependence on technology, sophistication and the ability to effectively wield against said country.

Towards that end, this chapter we will begin constructing a general baseline so as to help reasonably classify the technological capability of different countries, gain a general understanding of it then give a better initial step in deciding whether cyberwar would prove feasible based on the level of effectiveness offered.

Level I Countries: Level I countries are those with primitive to virtually no technological capability to speak of. In some cases this can amount to not even having the most basic of telecommunication capabilities or modernity, including not possessing the means to generate electricity. Examples of such countries abound, such as areas in parts of Africa and tribal groups in the Amazon.

Level I countries are those that by virtue of having little to no technology to speak of are also the least susceptible to any CW related attack. In some cases, even CW augmentation provides less in terms of force multipliers as the land itself provides natural barriers to the use of the electromagnetic spectrum. An example of this would be limitations to the HF spectrum in the jungle (Which was a prominent issue during the Vietnam War), or attempting to use Line of Sight communication tools where it is impossible to get an unimpeded view between two points. In countries of this variety, we occasionally see higher level technology such as solar panels, bicycle generators and so forth that have been introduced by foreigners to help societies that lack technological sophistication, however these are generally survival tools and not indicative of actual indigenous technological capability.

Internet availability is generally rarely available or non-existent. Though cyberwarfare can still provide some use against Level I countries, however not so surprisingly, the fact that there is little to no dependence on technology actually gives the country in question a natural advantage as there is simply nothing to target with cyber-based means. CW enhancements to units should be emphasized along with the force multipliers they bring along. (GPS, Infrared/Night Vision, Thermal, Laser-based, etc.)

Level II Countries: These are countries with minimum technological capabilities by modern day standards. Current examples of such countries would be modernized African countries, parts of South America and some of the more poor countries in Far Eastern Europe. There is a relatively consistent use of and reliance on modern technologies with a possible level of need and dependence on the convenience it provides.. Examples include electricity, television, radio, cellular phones, air conditioning and relative general availability of Internet access. (This can tend to involve the use of cybercafés due either how expensive it is for the population to pay for computers/Internet access at home or because of heavy government restrictions which necessitates it's use.)

Due the relative minimum amount of technology available, there is inversely less to target with CW. Cyberwar can be more effectively waged on countries falling into this category vice Level I due the ability to not only fight at a military level through CW augmentation, but because there are further means to disrupt technologies of convenience that would create more confusion in the civilian population and hinder the ability for the government to effectively provide information to them. Of particular note is the more likely widespread use of mass communication technology such as television, cell phones, landline phones and so forth which can be exploited and used for PSYOP purposes or completely shut down.

Level III Countries: Level III countries fit the more typical modern day definition of technological sophistication. Countries such as the Philippines or Mexico could fall into this category. The civilian population tends to have access to or possess most modern day technology, such as cellular phones and consistent electrical availability. A general ubiquity of Internet access will be available (through either pervasive Internet cafes or dial-up connections at home, along with scattered broadband availability) as well as automobiles and computers. A majority of the global community will fall into this category and provide a baseline to judge the other levels.

This level allows for all general methods and tactics available to cyberwarfare including shutting down web servers, banking systems, making the electromagnetic spectrum unavailable for use, supporting infrastructure, military targets and so forth.

Level IV Countries: Level IV is a level of advancement which would be a step up from Level III. This would be a level that many of the stronger nations in the world would fall into, such as Canada and Spain. These are countries with widespread use of nearly all forms of modern day technology. Internet access is widespread and available for all, including at homes of the general population. There will likely be technologically sophisticated hospitals, possibly world-class supercomputers and they will tend to already possesses at least some cyberwarfare capabilities. Level IV countries are able to mobilize technology to assist them in the basics of CW, get out information at an incredibly quick pace to people in their respective countries and generally are able to engage in cyberwarfare in some capacity at will.

Such countries will generally also have the capacity to conduct in depth research that can put them on the cutting edge of technological warfare. This capacity can be recognized based on layers of logical support that hold it up, such as financial strength and wherewithal along with a good education system that produces creative minds.

Level V Countries: Modern, State-of-the-Art nations will fall into this category. These are the heavy hitters and possess the vast majority if not all of modern day technologies. It is also likely that they will possess considerable cyberwarfare assets and capabilities at their disposal. Many such countries not only possess cyberwarfare capabilities but are also creating/have created actually cybersoldiers that can attack and ostensibly are developing/have developed attack vectors that were previously considered extremely difficult or impossible. (Tapping fiber optic lines, breaking encryption on remote drone feeds, anti-satellite weapons and so forth.)

Level V countries have a demonstrated capability to retain cutting edge capabilities and retain it for an extended period of time. These are countries with the demonstrated will, power, finance and motivation to be the best; therefore they are. Examples falling into this category include the United States, Britain, Russia and China.

Level X Countries: Level X countries are those who do not fit as easily into the categories previously listed. I believe that in some ways, Level X countries could possibly be considered more dangerous than even those who are Level V capable. Many cyber capabilities are usually geared towards computer hacking in particular and do not require traditional advanced training to learn. Because of the open nature of the Internet and how often it is possibly to learn new skills in engineering, computers science and virtually any other skill through reading ebooks and taking free online courses, it is essentially possible for any person with some motivation, an Internet connection or even an Internet cafe to make strides in catching up with others. This can impart surprises in terms of asymmetrical warfare as what was mistakenly labeled say a Level III country would in fact be able to accomplish much more.

A reasonable question could be posed regarding how it is possible that being a poorer country with vastly less resources and bereft of most modern day conveniences could actually have a greater potential for CW capability? The answer appears to lie in the fact that with at least a semblance of a steady Internet connection and the ability to collaborate with other knowledgeable people, this provides a strong amplifying effect on the spread of knowledge. For a country that is unable to afford billion dollar research budgets, world-class scientists or other such expensive projects, they can instead turn to gaining knowledge of technology and cyberwarfare as their new low cost, military arm of preference. Ebooks can be purchased at low cost (or pirated for free) and it is possible to pirate or purchase programs that teach languages, programming, different forms of engineering, entire university level courses on all forms of science and technology (Some coming from prestigious universities including MIT and Harvard) and literally have access to much of the best knowledge in the world. It is quite possible for one innovative spirit to set up an entire cyberwarfare command with nothing but a laptop, Internet connection, a tiny budget, inquisitive people and some ingenuity.

Because of the generally impoverished nature of Level X countries, the inverse effects of cyberwarfare become more readily apparent for a country without many technological conveniences/advances. The ability for a country to utilize cyberwarfare with relative impunity knowing that the opposing country will struggle to respond works well for said country. Further note lies in the fact that countries with greater technological sophistication are actually more vulnerable to such attacks and may not consider it fiscally feasible to respond in kind with cyberwar. Even worse, properly trained individuals can be sent to other countries with orders to conduct attacks, thus acting as plausible cover in case of possible implication of the home country involved. (Perhaps causing further consternation as to why sophisticated attacks are coming from an allied country or inside the host country itself.)

Some have already regarded these possibilities with mild amusement however the same critics would likely not be smiling at the case of 15 year old Thiago Olson in the United States. Thiago, using only materials bought from local stores/the Internet, college physics books and searching forums online managed to build a small nuclear reactor inside his parent's home.[29] With a strong innovative spirit along with the will and motivation to succeed at a new venture virtually anything can be accomplished.

Another issue which plagues highly sophisticated Level V countries yet works in favor of Level X lies in a fundamental poison which continues to strike down the most powerful countries who attempt to maintain their supremacy in the world: Complacency. When people are living comfortably with modern day conveniences then they fall into a sense of complacency and relaxation. After all, said

[29] Mone, Gregory. "Teen Builds Basement Nuclear Reactor." *Popular Science*. N.p., 20 Mar. 2007. Web. 17 Feb. 2014.

country feels as though they are at the top right? However, using the United States as an example, outsourcing would be a part of this complacency problem. Instead of growing talent organically at home, expertise is being exported at a cheaper cost overseas. Short term this translates into a healthier economy, however in the long term this creates a brain drain and makes the US beholden to the expertise that it refuses to cultivate. While the average American with a relatively healthy interest in computers may spend 8 hours a day learning a skill, there are very hungry and motivated programmers in more difficult to live countries that are learning at an exceptionally higher rate in comparison out of either need or a strong desire to learn. The lack of dependence on modern day convenience and technology in essence contributes to the abilities of individuals and a countries CW capability. We see this for example in North Korea.

Summary: As we begin drawing general guidelines regarding the technological capability of each country and classify them accordingly, a more detailed picture begins emerge regarding the level of effectiveness of cyberwar against different countries.

Of particular importance lies in the fact that we can also see why the current definition of cyberwarfare is quite inadequate. By confining the meaning to simply Internet or computer based terminology, it appears justified to simply cosign it to the generally lackluster corner of operations that cyberwar currently occupies. However as we can see through the country classification list, not only is an expanded definition necessary but also one that is all encompassing enough that we can begin seeing the future of full-spectrum cyberwarfare rather than the primitive organism it currently remains.

Chapter 3: Cyberwarfare Specialists

Advances in science and engineering continue to enable what was generally considered impossible only a few years before. 10 years ago, military grade lasers were considered mostly impractical, yet now they are being fielded on specifically modified planes, mounted on drones and slated for future use on US Naval warships. (Notably, Israel has recently fielded an advanced laser, nicknamed "Iron Beam" as part of its missile defense system, allowing low flying rockets to be shot down midair.)[30] Not too shabby for "impossible."

Though the creation of this technology has enabled humanity to advance considerably, unfortunately on the same token a side effect has been created: Global dependence on such technology has created a new center of gravity which can be attacked. To meet this threat, a new approach must be undertaken: A Cybercorps initiative. Staffed with specialists who rely on technical expertise, natural curiosity and an innovative spirit, it will be possible to create an unprecedented level of capability through the establishment of an agency staffed by computer

---

[30] "Israel Plans Laser Interceptor 'Iron Beam' for Short-range Rockets." *Reuters*. Thomson Reuters, 19 Jan. 2014. Web. 17 Feb. 2014.

specialists, hackers and other technically proficient, innovative individuals who will be charged with national cyberwar defense and providing support for military and civilian agencies in accomplishment of said charge. In this chapter we will be developing general guidelines on how such a specialized organization can be of benefit to a host country. Cybercorps will focus on not only technical training in their fields of expertise but also cross train with other government organizations to enhance their CW capabilities. In this book we will delve further in depth on how to apply CW capabilities in various forms of warfare, including Conventional, Unconventional, Guerrilla warfare, PSYOP and Intelligence operations.

Conventional Cybercorps- In general, all countries have some form of a standing military that is prepared to stand and protect its citizens from foreign invasion and to impose the will of their civilian leaders against other countries through warfare. Utilizing this logic, it follows that the development of a cyberwarfare agency which focuses on conventional CW operations will be necessary. It is important that in addition to general recruiting from the civilian community, different branches of the military are encouraged to cull their ranks for technically proficient and innovative individuals to support this new agency.

Resistance on such an endeavor that attempts to for all intents and purposes poach talent from different organizations should be expected depending on the political culture supporting that branch, therefore concessions should be offered to make such an exchange equitable. (For example, providing a certain level of support for each branch so all can see a benefit from supporting the stand-up of a Cybercorps.) There is a multiplicity of possible support options that such an organization can also provide for other groups such as law enforcement, disaster relief, protection of critical assets and so on however for the purposes of this book we will be focusing more specifically on cyberwar as it related to military and intelligence operation.

CyberCorps members are the lifeblood of this organization and without it, will undoubtedly fail. The focus on what is important must be watched over constantly: In cyberwarfare, technology is only as powerful as the intellectual force and innovative spirit in the person that wields it. As specialists and basic units of conventional CW operations, they will be individuals who will focus on all elements of full-spectrum cyberwarfare as previously defined. Successful individuals apart of this agency will tend to possess certain talents such as an innovative mind, a compulsive desire to achieve, perfectionism, competitive nature, technological expertise (via experience in engineering, computing, science, technology or if lacking credentials, a demonstrated ability through their personal interest) or particularly the ability to think outside the box. The popular conception is for many members to be people with traditional experience, such as individuals with computer security degrees and so forth. However, this is a paradigm which can only be partially adhered to assuming the new expanded definition of cyberwarfare. With new definition in hand, we see that the current way of thinking quickly expands and would require the incorporation of people who have experience with engineering, mathematics, technology, hacking, and many other disciplines. The main crux of virtually every discipline will be talents that are more difficult to ascertain, such as an innovative spirit, the ability to look at technology in a discerning manner and attempting to exploit it followed by the innate clairvoyance necessary to create new technology which others are not ready for.

The strength of this type of agency will lie in their ability to combine their respective knowledge bases in exploiting and leveraging technology to support operations at large. Cybercorps specialists will focus on not only utilizing this technology but also using a variety of means with an innovative spirit so as to exploit this technology to act in ways to which the creator likely did not intend. This spirit of innovation will also be used against foreign technology as to not only understand it, but also use it in ways to which they likely did not intend.

Generally, the country or group being moved against will be assessed into a technological category with CyberCorps units being utilized accordingly. This can be either through CW specialist teams with specific missions or by sending in mobile teams with support roles, such as sending specialists to augment and enhance conventional units that are already in the area of operations to repair equipment, support offensive operations against enemy units, work to deny the enemy the capability the use of their technological assets or disrupting civilian government control as possible examples. (Examples including use of government information dissemination tech, TV's, radios, cell phones, etc.) These units will also be used against the cybersoldiers of an opposing force as well, including hackers and other subversive elements.

 1) Attack- One of the aspects of battling in the field of technology and cyberspace will be an offensive capability that allows this specialized agency to fulfill its mission in supporting the government and military. There are a variety of methods and vehicles to move against different attack vectors. The attacking capability of the Cybercorps is limited only by the innovative spirit of the person engaging in CW and the limitations of technology itself. In general, the attacking role of the warfighter can include such actions as DDOS attacks, active electromagnetic denial of communications, (Including GPS, Satellite, Laser-based, etc.) exploiting technology and innovation to continue supporting operations.

The strength of cyberwarfare is particularly felt by a Cybercorps group which has a strong level of talent, funding and high level of innovation and technological sophistication. Many attribute the level of cyberwar capability more on the level of funding, or sophistication so as to decide as to whether a group or country is at from a power standpoint. However, the books necessary to fuel an innovative mind are plentiful, of little cost or in many cases as easy as walking to the local library and reading it for free. (Or at no cost through a variety of other means such as downloading pirated ebooks through the Internet, sharing ebooks to friends or even watching Youtube videos.) Because we are currently living in the Information Age, anyone with enough curiosity and motivation can find a book on virtually any topic for almost no cost at all and greatly increase what he is capable of. (Due our living in the Information Age, information has made human minds the true force multiplier.) Because of this, many times the power of attack or defense in a Cybercorps group is not so much related into how much money the group has or how good some of the software is but more of based on the level of talent the actual individuals possess.

An innovative, talented pool of people can push a Cybercorps group to a considerable level of strength at a proportionately smaller cost because of this very fact: Money and buying products does not create a powerful group, attracting good talent and innovative minds is paramount.

However there are different methods of attack for the strategic level to consider: For example, when fighting a technologically unsophisticated appoint, there are almost always levels of attack that can support the attacking force. The current paradigm is to confine cyberwar to mostly computer related enterprises however it is important to work towards ending this method of thinking and consider full-spectrum cyberwarfare instead. When speaking on full-spectrum warfare, we will again move away from purely computer or Internet based attacks and step towards real life operations, including shutting down or co-opting cellular networks, taking down TV signals/broadcasting with your own signal, temporarily cutting fiber optic cabling/satellite connections, etc.

Software-based attacks includes unauthorized attempts to access a computer system or the attempted insertion of pre-programmed code into another system so as to cause it to deviate from standard operation into a manner that the writer of said software desires. The only real limit to software based attacks is the available vectors for insertion, limitations of technology and the imagination of the writer himself. Some of the more common attack software types include viruses, malware, trojans, logic bombs, crafted attack tools, hacking attempts and so forth. Though there is application within the traditional methods of cyberwar, however its use in full-spectrum warfare is considerably more powerful.

One usually uses offensive software to attack computers, however within the vein of technology in general there is suddenly much more to attack. Virtually all technology that relies on any type of software in the world can be attacked through software based attacks, including cars, cell phones, traffic lights, or satellites. In the more traditional cyberwar train of thought, if one can keep their system away from the Internet then it is impossible to attack. Technology has moved at such a pace that even without an Internet connection it is still very easy to insert software or hack a system through USB,

Bluetooth, Wireless, or a variety of other outside methods. Recent evidence of this occurred when penetration testers who were testing corporate security began walking around and laying USB drivers around the building with malicious software loaded. Natural human curiosity took over, and employees picked up the USB drivers and actually plugged them into their computers. In general regards to software-based cyberwarfare attacks, the best policy is to take a mission or problem, allocate a timeframe and then allow subordinate cybersoldiers to figure out the best solution themselves. (Thus encouraging and relying on an innovation spirit to get the job done.) In Special Operations, a good measure of leadership is when a leader tells you what to do and allows you to figure out how to get it done, not use micromanagement and give robotic directions to follow, step by step.

Hardware-based: Hardware tends to be somewhat overlooked in comparison to software based attacks; however software without the hardware to support and run it is essentially the same as a car without an engine. Because of the importance of such systems for virtually any level of technology in the world, it is necessary to ruthlessly attack such support systems whenever possible. (It is noteworthy that moving against these types of systems also may require less technical capability, thus possibly making it more cost-effective in comparison to software based attacks.)

We will therefore spend some time answering the pertinent question of what should constitute hardware and its support systems and then discuss about theoretical ways to attack said systems.

The natural first question should be, "What counts as hardware?" Though generally this term tends to cover different computer devices, such as CPU's, hard drives and so forth, for the purposes of this book we are going to drastically expand the definition to also include communication systems, the mediums it travels through, computer networks connected locally or via the Internet, assorted transfer devices such as USB drives, DVD-ROM's, satellite dishes, wireless cards, Bluetooth connectors, modems, microwave dishes and their support systems, including electrical systems, water for water-cooled equipment and so forth.

Another question that should be asked and answered is what exactly is meant by "the medium it travels through?" The medium can essentially be considered something that is a facilitator of a path of data, which can include spaces as the electromagnetic spectrum such as Extremely High Frequency, Very High Frequency and Super High Frequency spectrums, microwave transmission frequencies, telephone lines for carrying data and fiber optic cabling or even simple copper cabling for the transmission of data. Recognizing the medium which data and information travel through as a valid area of operations will be helpful in preventing others from harnessing and taking advantage of it.

As we can see, moving against hardware systems, their support structures and the mediums that transmit information it is possible to deprive an opposing force of helpful or even critical force multipliers and other such necessary support structures. We will concern ourselves with two primary measures towards action, namely active and passive.

Active- These measures focus on forcefully attempting to deprive an opposing force of their hardware or support systems, usually in real time or in a manner which lacks subtlety. When conducting active attacks there will be less of a focus on covering up the origin of the attack but instead using lightning strikes. Such attacks can include automated hacking utilities onboard drones to take control of other drones in midair, anti-satellite weapons, directed energy weaponry, disabling cooling/electrical support systems, electromagnetic signal jamming equipment and so forth.

Passive- Passive methodology involves the sabotage of hardware components which are critical, or at the least important in the operation of a technological system. Passive HW attacks involve little to no participation on the part of the attacker and thus tend to rely on delayed measures of effect. Because of the general requirement of patience inherent in delayed tactics, these methods can require a level of patience. Examples of such passive hardware based attacks can include malware introduced into pre-fabricated chips at factories or purposefully including hardware defects that will eventually disable a device. In general, there is understood to be a tradeoff between active and passive tactics: Active is more forceful and immediate whereas passive provides more time to clean up and aid in preventing the possibility of discovering who the attacker is.

Real world examples of passive hardware-based attacks have already occurred, such as the speculated sabotage of the Trans-Siberian Oil pipeline which caused what was deemed the, "largest non-nuclear explosion in world history" of that time. A more recent example in news headlines, the National Security Agency was criticized for apparently intercepting packages being shipped to particular recipients that included pieces of technology, modifying it to meet mission requirements, boxing it back up and allowing the package to continue on to its intended destination.

In summary, with the rise of hacking, viruses and other such software-based attempts at moving against systems, the strength of a hardware based offense should not be underestimated. If one is able to disable the hardware for a system, then the system is effectively down. Of most importance lies in that the requirement for such high levels of technical expertise is not as necessary for accomplishing an attack, such as disrupting mediums.

2) Defend- The defensive capability of specialized units will prove to be another critical mission of the Cybercorps. Units will standby in their host country and continually work on improving their own skills, developing better security policy, creating better defensive software for protecting critical systems, recovering systems which have been hobbled by attacks and will prosecute a continuing mission emphasizing protection against hackers and those attempting to penetrate the defense of host nation systems. Attacks against technology will principally be defended through protecting against insertion points, hardening/protecting technology and aggressively pursuing human talent to out innovate the other side.

To help us meet this end we will break apart these concepts of defensive cyberwar into two categories: Software-based and Hardware-based planning.

Software-based: This level of defense will form the crux on which we will defend a country from cyberattacks. There is a considerable amount of perishable knowledge regarding this field as it evolves however there are some bedrock principles on which we can make basic assumptions, such as:

- The need to hire and retain talented, innovative individuals to craft good software.
- Hardening systems against outside attack.
- Creating a solid operating system.
- Developing proper defensive policies.

For the general computing field, there is a wide swath of tools and utilities to aid CW units, such as firewalls, anti-virus software, rootkit discovery, forensic tools and network analysis software among others. However for the most part, software-based defense is a saturated yet unsophisticated field. (The Windows operating system in particular has been almost continually maligned over a decade for its reputation of insecurity, yet virtually the entire US Military and Department of Defense still utilize this as their mainstay operating system.) Though major manufacturers of protection software make grand claims of defense and capabilities, for the most part these defenses can only hold the average hacker at bay. If one begins including well financed and supported hackers, or even a Cybercorps of their own then such software is the first to go down. For cyber defense, a more fundamental foundation must be laid so as to avert the constant need for software-based band aids.

There are many operating systems currently on the market, such as Windows and Linux. A general discussion on both is included below:

1) **Windows** tends to be the most user-friendly and well supported by the company that created it, Microsoft. It is also the most oft used, targeted and least secure. It is worth mentioning however that Windows has considerably improved the security of its software since early 2000, though another distinct problem lies in the closed nature of the system. An organization with a Cybercorps type setup cannot be dependent on an operating system manufacturer of who has a reputation for insecurity.

Crucially, the closed nature makes this type of software not only relatively useless for cyberwar specialists, but in many ways could be viewed as a liability. Though it is well known for its user friendliness, however the other side of the coin is that the OS is much easier to exploit and penetrate. Further, hackers are unable to examine and alter the core software as necessary to increase the defense strength of it along with the inability to craft a unique system which the average hacker or software tool cannot target with ease. In short, at this time Windows should be avoided as a mainstay operating system except for penetration testing purposes.

2) **Linux-** The best compromise between versatility and user friendliness, which can be adjusted as necessary depending on the flavor of Linux chosen. The critical difference that lies in this OS is the fact that it is an open, rather than closed system. This essentially means that anyone can download a copy of the software and makes changes to the core system as desired. Because of this, a unique

system can be crafted by the Cybercorps agency itself so as to provide better defense against well-known attacks along with a more imperceptible system which will help ward off ease of attacks common to other systems. A sense of pride and ownership can also be engendered, where CW specialists can begin crafting their "own" system of which they will feel a more vested interested in protecting. (Akin to defending ones house from outside attack.)

Therefore based on observation it appears that the best foundation for software defense is the creation of a unique, Linux-based operating system by Cybercorps members themselves. The next best option would be obtaining a relatively secure Linux distribution then moving to modify and make it as secure as possible for a first line of defense.

Thus far we have discussed the different methods for defending general computing systems, but what about other technology? Many of the same basic methods and rules remain applicable to all technology, ie the need for an open operating system to alter as necessary. There are currently, and for the foreseeable future, a multiplicity of different types and levels of technology throughout the world.

One might pose the question how can we possibly have a catchall software that fits every possible technology? The answer is that like every system that is targeted through cyberwar, they generally have the same logical composition: Hardware and dependent software that is manipulated through higher forms of software. (Such as Operating Systems.) The better developed the software/operating system, the more powerful the defense. (Java in particular has proven to be mobile and often used software for a good corner of the technology market such as TV's, ATM Machines and cell phones.)

Hardware-based: Based on the earlier hardware attack section it is possible to begin to scratch the surface at how debilitating these types of attacks can be. (Some of which can be accomplished with no computer expertise of any kind.) Along with setting reasonable safeguards in software and the operating system, adequate protection should also be provided for the hardware and transmission mediums necessary to allow the system to communicate. Therefore further consideration is warranted to defend against external attacks from this vector as well.

Properly protecting hardware is to be considered just as important as protecting the software. The fact of the matter is attacking through software means requires a certain level of technical expertise that is in short supply at the moment. Because of this, the current weak link in defeating an opponent with certain capabilities is to take the strategy of focusing on the hardware itself, which tends to not be particularly well defended. (It is essentially an attack vector where the best defenses offered are some security cameras and minimum wage security guards. Hardly a deterrent against a major attack.) Not to mention that it is much cheaper and easier to simply physically destroy a computer network or transmission medium rather than going through the software route, which requires much more expertise and time. However as enticing (and cheaper) it is to move directly against the physical portion of systems, it should be kept in mind that software methods can not only be much more subtle, but they can also be accomplished without a risk to life, mission planning, flying personnel around the world and so forth. Whether a direct attack or more subtle methods are needed will usually be dictated by what the requirements of the mission outcome are and the resources of the attacker themselves.

This list is by no means exclusive, however there are a variety of simple methods that are available to the attacker to protect physical systems, including improving physical security, tools limiting physical access, tempest shielding to help reduce or eliminate electromagnetic emanations, removing unnecessary connections from the Internet and providing sensors to detect tampering of cabling. Of further use are additional hardware-based equipment which provides capabilities for further defense, such as hardware-based firewall or servers with dedicated defensive software such as intrusion detection systems or honeypots.

Unlike previous suggestions for protecting, CW specialists should instead collaborate with other individuals to more adequately address security concerns with hardware. In some cases, it may be better to err on the side of caution and allow outside entities that specialize in physical security to instead safeguard their equipment. However in rare cases, some entities have already displayed the ability to adequately protect their own equipment within their facilities. (Such as the National Security Agency.)

Considerations/Recommendations: Usually when considering operations involving technology and computers, unconventional ideas tend to take the driver seat. And rightfully so, may I add. It can be used to cause considerable problems towards countries where there is a considerable proliferation and even dependence on technology. However despite these strengths, the limitations of such method are also apparent. Just as in traditional guerrilla warfare throughout history, one can only harass, pester and annoy the enemy without having a conventional force that can adequately protect infrastructure over a lengthy period of time, field training forces to have a steady stream of talent and provide levels of consistency that are needed for a long standing forces rather than one that hides in the bushes, conducts occasional attacks and vanishes. To this end, a standing centralized, conventional cyberwarfare center should be created to address this deficiency.

Attempts should be made to limit the "fracturing effect" that tends to happen in governments and military forces in regards to establishing a conventional agency. History is replete with examples of members of governments or the military attempting to create their own "personal force" rather than pooling resources to create a singular, most effective agency/group. For example, in the United States we see this problem in relation to intelligence: There is CIA intelligence, FBI intelligence, state police intelligence, DEA intelligence, NSA intelligence, Navy, Army, and Air Force intelligence, the Defense Intelligence Agency et all. The same disruptive fragmentation of the available brain pool is also unfortunately beginning to occur with cyber forces in the United States, with cybersoldiers specifically for the US Army, Navy, Marines, Air Force, Coast Guard, the NSA et al. The pool of talent is too thin to allow possibly a dozen agencies to spread thin a tiny group of people who are unable to provide as good assistance compared to all of them working together. (An excellent example of pooling great talent is

DARPA, who has also developed the reputation for being the best among the best among the security community.)

Chapter 4: Unconventional Warfare

"No one is so brave that he is not disturbed by something unexpected."

--Julius Caesar

Unconventional Cybercorp Specialist- In the area of unconventional warfare Cybercorp specialists will particularly shine. Generally, unconventional warfare organizations attempt to recruit highly motivated, intelligent individuals who are able to the think outside of the box. They are then given specialized training and provided with customized, expertly made tools with which to accomplish their mission. Due all of these force multipliers one can begin to form a vision to see how the UW specialist will be especially effective in unconventional warfare, who will be utilizing technology as the preeminent new force multiplier. It will be important to maintain a similar spirit of recruitment, namely finding personnel with technological expertise, an innovative spirit, motivated and willing to learn new technology. Depending on the role involved, elements of physical fitness will likely also become important. Unlike traditional unconventional operations however, the emphasis will be on technological expertise and the ability to innovate and solve problems in support of operations rather than being at the height of physical strength. Rather the emphasis should be on reaching the height of intelligence and innovation. When a motivated individual is equipped with technological knowledge and deployed to other countries, the level of chaos that can be caused is incalculable. In addition, stronger levels of support can be laid for conventional forces, intelligence agencies and later UW assets. It is important to understand that though one could attempt to train currently existing unconventional warfare units in different aspects of cyberwar rather than use conventional cyberwar specialists, however the effectiveness will be greatly reduced as compared to a dedicated, continuously training asset who has a natural interest in computing and technology.

In this section we will be going over some of the elements of operational support that UW specialists can provide, including in Special Operations, Counter-Guerrilla Warfare, Psychological Operations and Intelligence

Special Operations- There is certain missions which require a level of expertise and/or discretion that cannot be reasonably accommodated by conventional forces. Of the missions that are known by the public, these are usually the type which tend to be exceptionally dangerous and require unusual levels of expertise such as training foreign forces, conducting operations in advance of conventional invasions or covert methods necessary to support country interests. To this end, small groups of skilled, innovative troops will be employed to accomplish these difficult tasks. Members of Cybercorp Special Operations units will apply this same mentality towards cyberwarfare however unlike the general special operations community, there will be a slight shift in focus away from traits such as peak physical strength and instead give a stronger emphasis on traits such as exceptional technical expertise in technology, strong understanding of computers and working knowledge of communication technologies. Other traits will also be highly valued, such as a desire for continuing awareness of current technology available, future advances in technology and the ability to think out of the box and engineer uses out of basic technology that it was not initially intended for. There tends to be a general reaction to these types of requirements by emphasizing traditional education, such as university level training, however this should be kept in perspective: Though one can be highly educated and knowledgeable, greater emphasis on USO's (Unconventional Specialist Officer) will rather be on the ability to innovate, a hunger to learn and a desire to understand the technological world. Rote, memorized knowledge should be granted a lower level of emphasis than previously mentioned traits.

Now with a basic foundation on what type of traits a successful USO will possess has been laid we will next discuss different areas in which technology can best be leveraged to support special operations.

Infiltration/Support- In a world growing further dependent on technology, there continues to be a growing potential for the use of new and emerging tech to aid in the infiltration and support of infiltration of USO's into target countries. Some of the different methods of aid include:

Covert Funding: This can be currently accomplished through alternative crypto currency software such as Bitcoin. Bitcoin[31] is an emerging digital currency which has no international monitors and thus allows the covert movement of money of any amount virtually

---

[31] Biddle, Sam. "What Is Bitcoin?" *Gizmodo*. N.p., 19 Mar. 2011. Web. 17 Feb. 2014.

anywhere in the world at any time. With this software, a "digital wallet" is created, encoded and can be accessed anonymously from anywhere in the world. Because of a lack of any identifying information to obtain this wallet, (it is created through locally downloaded software) it is currently near impossible to identify owners of said accounts who follow some basic security procedures. With a digital wallet, the ability to covertly moved money is limited only by the imagination. Digital wallets can be encrypted/password protected and put on USB drives, hidden on laptops, sent via email, digitally encoded onto websites, put on cellphones and so forth. Utilizing technology such as this, it is possible to covertly move large amounts of money to support operations anywhere in the world as one is limited only by the size of a file which is only a few megabytes.

The following example provides a good fictionalized, real world use of digital currency in support of operations would be this: Suppose I am the leader of a Special Operations unit that has been tasked with providing covert guerrilla support in a foreign country. While in country, the funding command could encode $10,000,000 into a Bitcoin account, use sophisticated encryption programs that are publicly available such as PGP or Truecrypt to protect it, and finally make the file available on a commonly used website. I can then go to said public website, retrieve the encrypted account, input the necessary password and then begin using various methods to exchange Bitcoins into local currency. Again, the methods of moving these digital wallets are limited only by the imagination itself.

Because digital crypto currency is still in its infancy there is a generally inherent lack of legislation that would hinder money laundering thus making the prefect vehicle for moving money. Because of this there is a much greater ability to move massive amounts of funds around the world with little to no oversight and thus can more effectively support operational funding without the fear of arousing suspicion.

Encryption Software: The ability to move information without fear of discovery is important. Though military grade software or hardware can generally fit many mission requirements, however this type tech tends to be less than user friendly or bulky, thus making it less helpful in supporting special operations. Commercial grade encryption software seems to fit this use in a much more user friendly manner while seemingly providing even greater encryption capabilities. There are a multitude of different types of software that can be used to support requirements for secure communications for the Special Operations community depending on the type of communication needed. Below is a list of types of possible types of commercial of the shelf (COTS) encryption that can be utilized based on current day software:

Voice: One of the more common mediums of transferring information. Having a method of conducting secure voice communications can be very helpful. Thanks in part to greatly advanced VOIP software and portable PBX tech, it is now possible to field voice encryption in the field that is lightweight, relatively user friendly and more importantly does not stand out to the general public. In terms of software, there remains a slew of different publicly available software that allows for encrypted voice communications. Examples include PC/Mobile based software such as Skype, which offers 256bit AES encrypted voice calls.[32] Another type of software would include "Silent Call" which allows encrypted voice communications between iPhones. Additional there are hardware solutions that are already becoming available as well, such as "TrustCall" which provides 256bit AES encrypted voice calls via an iPhone by simply inserting a small encryption chip into the memory card slot. Even without encryption software, it is still possible to make relatively safer calls than with landline/cellular phones by instead using smartphones which are wireless capable. Upon connecting via wireless to a public access point (Which can be a nearby McDonalds, Starbucks, or even wireless access from a nearby residence.) it is possible to attempt to reply on security through obscurity and use either open wireless access points or those whose passwords have been cracked, then making a phone call through the wireless connection to land lines or other cell phones. As software and hardware becomes faster, lighter and more powerful we will continue to see stronger, more lightweight encryption that is continually at ones fingertips at all

---

[32] As of recent times Skype is less secure due its new owner, Microsoft displaying a ready willingness to produce information it has recorded thus rendering encryption less helpful.

times. It will also be available for all to use via the Internet or at a local store near you.

Video: As cheap bandwidth continues to increase, there is also a correspondingly enhanced communications ability that would have been prohibitive in times past or the benefits to justify the necessity did not exist. One of these capabilities is face to face video chat. Through face to face video chat, it is possible to engage in conversation through a method that before required extensive planning, hardware and overcoming problems with compatibility. (Assuming not everyone was using the same type of virtual teleconferencing software.) However thanks to advancements in COTS software, we not only have publicly available face to face video software but it also allows for group teleconferencing with multiple video feeds and also the ability to conduct encrypted chat. The USO should continue to keep abreast of current software and provide further enhancement of software/hardware solutions so as to continue to allow this capability in the field.

Some methods of conducting encrypted video chat are enabled by publicly available and free software such as Skype and Jitsi. Skype in particular, as with voice based chat, allows one to make face to face video calls through ones PC, on cellular phones, or for best security by turning off the cellular capabilities of a cell phone (Usually be turning on some type of Airplane Mode) and then connecting via wireless to make the call.

Innovation and exploiting publicly available technology continues to be of importance. One example of being able to conduct via videos is the use of publicly available video sharing sites, such as Youtube. It is possible to create and make publicly available videos which seem harmless and typical while it carries particular gestures or other methodology involving code so as to transmit messages. This is a method of "hiding in plain view" which allows the transmission of messages with relative confidence.

One of the fortunate and unfortunate aspects of technology is that knowledge becomes perishable at an incredible rate. Many books are written on computers and technology with a focus on perishable knowledge, then quickly become obsolete as time marches on. Of course there are other methods available to release video messages as well.

Email: Email has been the mainstay of communications for over a decade. Through it the world has been able to communicate at little to no cost in an easy, efficient format. Encrypted messages sent via email have nearly just as long of a history, being used to send sensitive messages from around the world. There are such a vast amount of different types of publicly available, virtually unbreakable encryption as of this writing that it will suffice to suggest only a cursory search of the Internet to find software that will fulfill mission requirements in regards to secrecy. The veritable Pretty Good Privacy(PGP) software deserves a mention,, which is generally considered the industry-wide standard for protecting data. Email is slowly becoming the new snail mail of our age however. With the rapid introduction of newer, faster technology such as text messaging and online messengers along with their quick adaption by communities around the world, there has been a marked decrease in the use of email. (Though intranet messaging inside of businesses tends to be fairly constant.) Countries such as the Philippines, for example, heavily use cellular texting as the prime method of communication.

General Data: For the needs of general data we can use encryption software such as Truecrypt.[33] With Truecrypt it is possible to create encrypted, digital containers so as to allow one to store information inside it with confidence. The encrypted containers are virtual in nature and prove a considerable barrier to retrieval of any kind without knowledge of the password. Attempts at cracking said software is also extremely difficult, despite repeated attempts from authorities worldwide. A multiplicity of possible options in deciding how to use this container is available, such as the storage of scanned documents, storage of emails, bitcoin wallets, private correspondence and so forth.

Publicly available encryption has reached the point that even well financed, world-renown organizations are struggling to decrypt it. One recent example of this was the inability of the Brazilian National Institute of Criminology being unable to

---

[33] http://www.truecrypt.org/

decrypt the hard drive of a Brazilian businessman that was under investigation. After a lengthy and failed attempt, they passed the hard drive onto the Federal Bureau of Investigation in the United States. Despite the FBI running a dictionary cracking program for over a year on the hard drive, they too were unable to decrypt it and retrieve the information necessary.[34] This was a public display of the staggering difference in the ability of federal police agencies to decrypt information as compared to the ability of others to encrypt it.[35]

Text-Based Chat: Real time chat continues to a simple, versatile tool for transmitting information around the world at virtually no cost at all. Primary methods of chat include front end tools such as Internet Relay Chat (IRC) or through web-based chat, such as Yahoo chat. Methods of transmitting secret information are simple as well, either through the use of code, chat clients that encrypt text on the fly or via

---

[34] "FBI Hackers Fail to Crack TrueCrypt." *TechWorld*. N.p., 30 June 2010. Web. 17 Feb. 2014.

[35] The fact that the FBI used a dictionary cracker for over a year is instructive. If a password can't be found within a short amount of time via a dictionary cracker then it would likely be much better to attempt brute forcing instead. The time spent running a dictionary cracker that long is akin to the fabled hunt for Pancho Villa.

innocuous intermediary tools. Intermediary tools are those which have a legitimate purpose while only providing chat as an ancillary tool to encourage better gameplay. These types of information transmission only require an innovative mind to conceive relaying information, such as through online PC games (World of Warcraft, Yahoo Chess), stock trading sites, or perhaps media console games. (Such as Xbox, Playstation or Nintendo multiplayer online chat.) It can be clearly seen that there is a considerable ability to hide in plain view through simply finding software/hardware that is being mass produced and used, then transmitting said messages through that digital medium.

Falsified/Modified Passport Smartchips: The ability to falsify passports has become the trademark of virtually every country and of criminal organizations, and times haven't changed in the information age. This tradition has continued from the used of forged papers in World War II to the digital passport chip technology of today. Virtually any country can utilize modified or completely fake passports so as to all the surreptitious entry of forces into foreign or even enemy countries. To continue this tradition of covert entry, it is also possible to use emerging technology such as passport chips to aid entry. As technological sophistication continues to grow we can also portend a possible future in which nearly all biometric and personal information can be encoded on passport chips in a similar manner to which information is encoded on credit cards. Therefore with the continuing pervasive use of passport chips it will become continually easier to covertly insert forces into foreign countries through legitimate means of travel such as boat, air, or by rail.

Of course there will be naysayers who proclaim how secure their chips are and how it would take 1 million+ years to crack their passport information etc, however they will have merely continued a nasty trend of underestimating how much can be accomplished by a young, innovative mind with nothing to do but sit around, attempting to accomplish something considered cool or noteworthy from home. (Not to mention entire teams of specially trained personnel with a financial budget supporting by the military, a government or other individual/corporations with large pockets.)

Communications: The ability for a USO to communicate in different environments is limited only by his knowledge and innovative spirit. Particular points of knowledge that will prove useful include an understanding of electromagnetic wave propagation, electrical engineering and computer technology. Knowledge should be shaped around the ability to communicate across any medium including radio wave, satellite, cellular and Internet-based communications using every day products which can be purchased without arousing suspicion.

One such method of covert communication involves the cracking, and use of wireless signals which belong to other entities such as businesses, other people and so forth. Publicly available software such as Aircrack-ng[36] enables the USO to capture signals from wireless routers, deduce encrypted passwords and thus allow surreptitious access to another's Internet. Of course this enables other possibilities such as network intrusion, DDOS attacks

---

[36] http://www.aircrack-ng.org/

and so forth which can create even more opportunities for covert, protected communications.

Disrupt Internet- The main focus in this type of mission will be disrupting or completely shutting down a countries Internet. The Internet provides many conveniences throughout the world; including helping disseminate information and providing ease of communications to others between different areas. Though the Internet is built to be resilient against attack however this does not infer that it is completely impervious to the serious minded attacker.

Centers of gravity that prop up Internet based communications should be identified and neutralized either via software, hardware or physical means. A few examples of centers of gravity can include Internet Service Providers, government providers of Internet service, satellite providers, cellular providers and underground/underwater fiber optic lines. Disrupting methods of communicating via the Internet can be accomplished through either traditional methods of physically attack of nodes of access, (ISP's, government buildings, satellites, cutting fiber optic lines or the electrical pulsing of phone telephone lines) or by using software based methodology to shut down the source. (Distributed Denial of Service attacks, viruses or hacking are good choices for taking them offline.)   The general goal is using any means possible to cut a group/country off from being able to communicate locally or to the world grid via Internet means.

Disrupt Government services- A gradual shift continues from paper based government operations to electronic means as the march of the information age carries on. The shift from paper to electronic medium tends to encompass operations such as record keeping, information dissemination and communications due the exceptional convenience and cost effectiveness it provides.

The USO should aggressively target this center of gravity with the focus being on disrupting critical government operations at the local, state/provincial and nationwide level. Other pillars of strength to target include all electronic systems that help support government operations, such as attempting to destroy critical government electronic records, shutting down communications (TV, Radio, Telephone, Backups,

Websites, Email, Internal network systems), disrupting local infrastructure and support systems (Police, Emergency Medical services, Traffic lights) or beacons of economic activity such as stock exchanges.

Disrupt Military- As with other centers of gravity, the military naturally follows as another target. Though there tends to be higher level of security in general however it is often the case that militaries tend to lag behind (in some cases far behind) what the commercial market can offer in terms of computer security. There are some exceptions to this rule such as the case with the United States DARPA Agency however this is not the standard.

As the general theme of this book, the further reliance on technology in every facet of life including the military proves to be both a boon and the proverbial Achilles heel. Because of the specialized and focused nature of the military, it is important to put more effort into properly categorizing, mapping and attacking both networks and technology. In general, militaries such as that of the United States tend to benefit tremendously from a reputation of superiority in particular regarding technology. However as with any story, reality tends to reflect a quite different story than legends which are passed around. Giving appropriate note of reputation in the name of caution is advised, however they should be looked at carefully to see if justified and if not, then ignore them to focus on destroying the targets technological capabilities.

Categorization will be essentially similar to that of country classification codes assigned to countries. The military will be broken into all of its separate parts (Army, Navy, Marines, Air Force, Special Operations, Mercenaries, Support etc.) and then analyzed to determine their technological capabilities and how to go about disrupting, or possibly even terminating them in the most cost effective fashion possible. The technological reliance of the military being targeted will be of primary importance so as to adequately get the best "bang for your buck." (And also gain a better understanding at how effective cyberwarfare will actually be against the target.) With a firm understanding of who will be targeted, a general understanding of their technological capability and what results are desired then USO specialists can move in and attack from virtually anywhere in the world depending on what is being targeted and the nature of its security.

Some may find solace in a system that is completely removed from the Internet, however even security of that nature is never completely secure. Computers have manners of entry into systems that do not rely on the Internet for access such as CD-ROM's, USB Drives, keyboards which possess hardwired keyloggers, drones that can be hacked into, satellites that can be sabotaged, jamming communication networks and so forth. Even far flung targets are accessible, as warships tend to have constant satellite communications or even worse, are connected to the Internet 24 hours a day, 7 days a week. Many naval warships are connected to the Internet continuously while even submarines occasionally connect to satellites to download email!

The scope of cyberwarfare as it pertains to the military is large and significant as countries contend to become the most technologically advanced. It is my intention however to only cover some emerging layers of cyberwarfare with broad strokes so as to give a more general understanding.

Disrupt Infrastructure- The necessity for proper, functioning infrastructure is the hallmark of every country with any level of influence in the world. It allows the populace to live more securely and comfortably within their society while providing more time to complete tasking's and in many ways provides considerable value to who it serves. And just as militaries and Special Operations troops have targeted this infrastructure to fulfill mission requirements, so must the USO. A particular advantage that the USO holds is the fact that he can easily conduct operations from anywhere, anytime without typically having to carry around any specialized equipment and instead rely on tools which can be locally purchased nearby or built from scratch. Of course there are exceptions to this rule as with any other as there can be practical limitations depending on the country level. Finding the tools necessary to shut down a British satellite while sitting in a Level I area such as the Amazon jungle without outside support could prove difficult.[37]

Targets will include infrastructure which has any type of technological function including electrical power distribution plants, cellular towers, water filtration plants or pushing for lower grade attacks to add pressure on a government which is already struggling. This can include not only traditional targets such as electrical and water but also less conventional, such as stock trading markets, airports, seaports, oil producing stations, MWR facilities for military personnel, etc.

Disrupt Economy- The lifeblood of every country starts with the economic pillars which support it. There are multiple facets that support the pumping of this economic blood such as the global import/export infrastructure, high speed stock exchange trading, credit card processing and so forth. Economic centers of gravity are particularly vulnerable to cyberwarfare as the globe has strongly shifted to an almost universal focus and dependence

---

[37] Unless you are perhaps a member of the Gilligan's Island cast.

on using global networks, including the Internet to process transactions.

The effectiveness of economic warfare is particularly dependent on factors such as the countries dependence on forms of an electronic infrastructure, the economic strength of the host country conducting operations, economic strength of the target country and ability of the operator. It is also important to understand that there are few targets as well protected as the national and particularly the global infrastructure in terms of finance thus no particularly "nuclear" one shot attack should be considered particularly helpful. (Unless perhaps a terrorist organization had the ability and desire to send shockwaves throughout the world, such as by gaining complete, extended control of a major stock exchange/bringing it offline.) However the repercussions from such an attack which again send shockwaves throughout the world and are generally unhelpful, along with the fact that such an attack would be enormously difficult to accomplish.

Because of the disproportionate strength of the fighter in relation to defenders of the economic infrastructure he is to attack, it will be necessary to employ a guerrilla strategy involving "death by a thousand cuts" to antagonize and annoy a country. As with other methods of attack, this will involve locating and identifying centers of gravity that are both in finance, and undergird it which are dependent on some form of technology. Once the crosshairs have been aimed, then the USO will begin chipping away at the system with attacks that focus on low cost, high reward tactics.

a) **Devalue Trust in the System:** Inherent in any economic system is a certain level of trust which is important in keeping operations open. If people are depositing money in banks, buying stocks through a local exchange or even using credit cards/ATM machines, there is a certain trust relationship that the consumer has with the financial institutions themselves. The people trust that the bank will give them back their money when they desire, stocks can be sold when they no longer want them and so forth. The USO must work to undermine this trust in the system and create instability, causing a level of discomfort within the populace and by extension the financial institutions and the government. When the public begins withdrawing their money from bank accounts or discontinues using credit cards and buying as often, this can cause a domino effect which will discourage buying, provides less money for financial institutions to use themselves and also work towards depriving the government of a stronger overall economy.

One avenue of devaluing public trust would be commandeering publicly available news sources online that are well known and trusted then disseminating derogatory economic information to hurt companies, financial institutions or the government. (Including websites and social media.) Not only would this erode trust in news organizations but also has the ability to play havoc with different factors in stock markets prices and other economic areas. Though this could be used as an attempt to damage the economic market itself, smaller, less defended targets could be more effective and cost effective such as corporations or local businesses.

There are many ways in which one can attempt to reduce trust that the public or corporations have in the system however USO's should work in concert specifically so as to more effectively undermine the system as a whole.

b) **Currency Manipulation:** Due to government controls, any level of outside currency manipulation is extremely difficult without large amounts of money or considerable government support. Though it is in theory possible to use significant financial leverage to shift the value of currency up or down, however governments tend to have a diverse set of strong tools[38] to directly manipulate currency value and correct problems problem relatively quickly.

Despite the considerable sway a government has over its national currency, technology continues to act as a hobbling factor in a fast growing economy. Depending on the technological sophistication of the country, it may still be possible to cause problems with the currency of a country through various means such as attacking electronic financial holders

_____

[38] Commonly referred to as capital controls.

themselves, such as all-electronic arbitrage traders. These types of trades attempt to make profit by exploiting the price difference of a thing in one country vice its price in another country.[39] Through the use of high speed trading computers which can make trades in a matter of milliseconds, it is possible to make a profit. After millions of such trades, profits can measure up quickly.

This technological Achilles heel allows the possibility of breaking into such a system by insiders who could insert malicious software which could cause substantial damage within an incredible rate of time. (See Flash Crashes.) In addition to causing problems with high speed trading, it is also worthwhile to consider hacking as an option to causing problems from a software standpoint in such all-electronic arbitrage institutions, such as viruses or other malware which would destroy financial records. As previously demonstrated through inadvertent flash crashes, a forced flash crash could have serious consequences.

---

[39] Commonly referred to as arbitrage.

c) **Stock Exchanges:** Stock exchanges form of major economies around the world and are a central center of gravity that can devastate an economy if undermined. Examples of such devastating crashes are plentiful; including the 2008 Housing Crisis in the United States which caused a serious recession lasting years. Multiple flash crashes have occurred in which algorithmic errors in organization computers managed to wipe out trillions of dollars of money in minutes. Though crashes of such significant magnitude are likely not as easy to accomplish for the foreseeable future via cyberwarfare, (nor desired, as previously discussed, such an indiscriminant attack could cause widespread economic chaos throughout the world) however it is possible to utilize a more surgical approach to weaken the knees of an economy a bit.

Though countries have many rules in place to attempt to stop the manipulation of stock exchanges, it is not only difficult to enforce such rules but grows increasingly difficult as systems trend towards becoming more electronic based and faster than ever before. Insider trading has been and will continue to be a mainstay of stock markets, though attempts will continue to be made to stymie the issue as much as possible.

Looking at how to attack systems which are fairly strong from an outsider viewpoint can be daunting however the issue must be approached in a similar manner as other problems: Every system is only as strongest as the weakest human link, therefore the main questions should be how to strike and is it feasible? Granted any system can be broken in some manner, however the cost that would be required to conduct such an attack may not be worth the rewards reaped. It is possible to attack the stock exchanges themselves, however considering the critical nature of such systems and the effects they could have on the world economies, it is safe to say that they all likely possess some of the greatest security in the world against any level of cyberwar. (In general, even excluding major exchanges, considerable effort is put into the level of security of any exchange as trust is important. (See previous section on Devaluing Trust.))

However we can instead adopt guerrilla style tactics and ignore the large, well-protected base to instead move against the smaller, less protected electronic bases that help prop up the markets. Examples include the previously mentioned all-electronic arbitrage companies and holding companies. Other examples of the applicability of cyberwar in attempting to disrupt stock markets include the use of social media manipulation to temporarily cause markets to move up or down. When trusted news organizations Twitter accounts were hacked, false information was sent out which sent stocks crashing upon seeing negative information being repeated throughout the world and other large news networks. (Thus increasing the likelihood of the bogus information being attributed as believable.) This can be used either to make money in an expedient way, such as buying stock in the targeted companies enemies which will likely rise, or other such methods or allow temporary confusion which will allow other attacks to be conducted. As we can see, just as with any type of warfare, the more powerful, debilitating levels of cyberwar require in general an investment in time, money and personnel capable of conducting such an attack. However as with all electronic systems, nothing is completely secure.

   d) **Banks:** Banks, like stock exchanges are considered a virtual Fort Knox of security and rightfully so. Trust is important in such an institution, thus they invest heavily in protecting their clients' money so that more will be placed in the system. When depositors begin withdrawing money in large sums at a fast pace after that trust is removed, then we see the banks themselves panic and economies begin to shiver. (The Great Depression in the United States along with the public's reaction to the recent financial crisis in Cyprus and Greece show how economically deadly this can be.)[40]

Internet based attacks are possible however this is akin to storming the front gates of a military base which is on high alert and attack attempts are being made virtually every day. Though not impossible to storm the gates, the wiser course of

---

[40] Morici, Peter. "The Insanity of the Cyprus Crisis." *CNBC*. N.p., 28 Mar. 2013. Web. 17 Feb. 2014.

action would be to consider other attack vectors. One example would be to consider ignoring global scale banks such as Goldman Sachs and instead target regional banks or credit unions, which considering their smaller footprint and less name recognition are not as likely to have as strong defenses or to prepare as adequately as the bank with gigantic budgets.

As attacks from the Internet seem to currently be more difficult or simply infeasible (Electronic security is well done enough that the benefits do not often seem to outweigh the effort put in) it is either necessary to conduct attacks through the inside or by attempting to devalue trust in the bank itself. Insider attacks are considerably easier than from the outside as the insider obviously already has access to systems which the public does not. Of particular desire would be moving insiders into the IT departments or security so as to access major systems themselves and begin causing havoc. Even if the attacks themselves are not successful in toppling, or even making much a blip on the banks radar, however if the media gets ahold of said story then it immediately breeds doubt in the minds of depositors of said bank. "How can they let this happen?" is the words that will flash in their minds.

Another form of insider attack that can be considered is compromising the actually insiders that can shift stock prices in a significant way themselves. This can be accomplished through targeting the insiders email accounts, searching through corporate intranet messages and email or intercepting critical chat messages. This can enable either the ability to manipulate the person who can influence stock prices or provide the opportunity to pass on the information to the host country running the operation to act accordingly. (In possible cases of economic terrorism.)

If it is not possible or feasible to move insiders into the system or somehow influence insiders/gain access to the inside system, then a direct attempt at corroding trust in the bank will be necessary. The media and the Internet will likely be helpful, with attacks focusing on making said target appear inept, lazy, unable to protect their assets or their clients, pervasive corruption and so forth. This can be done through a variety of methods such as revealing damaging internal memos, exposing repulsive, immoral actions taken by bank leadership including through the uncovering of CEO's or CFO's damaging electronic records[41] and in general attempting to make the bank look like a less than safe place for others to place their money.

e) **Business:** Businesses are the low hanging fruit for cyber-attacks. Though the proportionality of security generally rises depending on the size and technological sophistication of the business, there are many ways to cause considerable problems for different organizations. Publicly traded companies have stocks which can have deadly effects if sufficiently lowered (See Devaluing Trust/Stock Exchange) or as with banks, insiders can destroy financial records, employee records and in general completely corrode a company from the inside out. In some cases it is possible to destroy entire companies that rely on electronic records and do not have the proper electronic or physical

---

[41] Email, text messages, phone calls, cell phone records, etc.

backups. (Or one could actually corrupt electronic backups as well!)

Technology is necessary for such organizations to compete and remain their main center of gravity. It is the attackers good fortune that that unlike banks, businesses tend to have a greater web presence and much lower security thus one can attempt to conduct outside penetrations in obtaining information of a damaging nature.[42] Fraud is another weapon in the USO arsenal, which can help in financing further ventures to support his ultimate aim, such as buying products with stolen/fraudulent credit cards online, abusing gift cards to purchase necessary products, etc. The possibilities remain limitless.

f) **Credit Cards:** As of this writing, credit card fraud is an expensive and serious problem. Billions of dollars are lost every year through a variety of schemes, even to the point that people are able to purchase fraudulently obtained credit information online, then use it

---

[42] Financial records, upcoming products to be released, confidential patents, proprietary information, etc.

to purchase necessary material online. Though this type of use may not prove helpful in economic warfare itself, however it is helpful for helping to illicitly fund operations when it is either not possible or not feasible for USO's to receive the funding needed to complete an operation.

The well-traveled way of obtaining such credit card information revolved around simply stealing said card, however that tends to be unhelpful as many people simply report the card stolen and it is turned off fairly quickly. Even worse, cameras tend to be in any store that one could use the card at and is a mainstay of virtually all ATM's. (If objects are purchased online, then they can be traced fairly quickly so as to ascertain where it is being purchased.)

For the common criminal this may be something that is not really much to be concerned about, however as one who is attempting to maintain a level of discretion while conducting covert operations this would be exceedingly unhelpful. Instead, it is better to either obtain cards through illicit means such as fake ATM machines (Which require surprising little difficulty to create) or simply obtaining one through online black markets. Millions of such cards are available online, of which the vast majority are not aware that the card was even stolen. Though one would still leave a digital trail from buying things online, however more importantly it allows more precious time to purchase an item online and receive it before the card is reported and tracked. More importantly, for every 1 card stolen with some effort, hundreds of thousands can be purchased for little effort or cost.

Hiding- Hiding has become increasingly difficult in the digital age. Not only is this in part because of the ubiquity of use, but also that through simple non-use it makes one stand out. With highly accurate satellite imagery, the pervasiveness of cameras and general better equipped surveillance than in the past, the inherent risks have increased gradually over the decades. With this in mind, techniques and ways of managing ones presence on the grid in proportion to need is helpful.

With the current state of technological surveillance, something as simple as a small color camera can be installed at a small gas station or sophisticated enough to watch entire nations. As one can be so easily watched in this digital age, it becomes incumbent on the USO to remain continually acquainted with current and future technology which could be used to detect him and know how to reasonably avoid such detection. This includes use of any type of technological device, regardless of sophistication. Different types of electronic trails that could be left should be scrutinized, including the possibility of CCTV, Internet usage, Credit Card usage, ATM's, high-profile areas with significant surveillance (Banks, Police stations, secure facilities, areas outside embassies, etc.)

Technological knowledge and remaining aware of one's surroundings and digital trail can prove useful in reducing the possibility of being discovered or leaving an electronic trail, depending on the country level being moved into. Examples of technology that can aid those engaging cyberwarfare include the use of metapaper to inhibit wireless signal use, Faraday Cages to largely reduce electromagnetic emanations, thermographic camouflage to cover up heat signatures of individuals or entire rooms, commandeering the wireless signals of other people to use for anonymous Internet usage, using areas with free internet (while keeping mind that there are likely local surveillance systems installed within the business of course), conducting Internet usage through secure satellite connections and so forth. The application of knowledge and common sense remains the easiest way to protect oneself.

Counter-tech (Anti-Cyberwarfare)- With technology as the primary target, mobile Countertech teams will be helpful in disrupting or permanent disabling an opponent's technology. Though as with most cyberwarfare, the mindset tends to only cover computer based systems however it is important to keep our mindset shifted towards the next level: Utilizing any means whatsoever to destroy their technology. This can include software based means, such as using malware/viruses and classic hacking to targeting infrastructure dependent on technology (Electricity, Water or Communications), businesses (See Economic Warfare), or even militaries. (Destroying classified information, subverting systems dependent on technology, erasing records or causing havoc with procurement systems)

A mobile Counter-tech team has many advantages at their disposal. Considering that only a small group of people can be used to have devastating effects, it will be easier to infiltrate said team into any country in the world and cause disproportionate effects. Further, the teams can also remain in country for an extended period of time while continually using surreptitious means to sabotage, disable, and otherwise harass the opposing force in their own homeland. Funding such a team will also be easier as it may be possible to avoid traditional means of providing financing, and instead using newer forms of alternative currency such as Bitcoin, Litecoin and so forth. These trained hacker teams will use every computer/technological tool at their disposal to cause havoc, including via electromagnetic pulse technology, cutting fiber optic cabling, using microwaves to damage satellites, viruses, DoS attacks, misleading attacks, etc. The main goal will be using any means possible to disable or destroy an opponent's technology behind enemy lines and if the best continue to be recruited, the results will be spectacularly in comparison to the size of the team.

Advanced Preparation for Conventional- When moving against an opposing country, covert forces are generally sent in beforehand so as to attempt and soften the field while attempting to help prepare for incoming forces along with moving towards hindering residing forces and hampering the government's capabilities. This tends to includes Special Operations troops, intelligence agencies and other support units. The future lies in new forward deployed units with superior technical capability such as USO's, who can also be fielded as mobile forces which will move in advance along with other forward deployed elements.

USO forces that have already inserted into a country in advance would be helpful in preparing to disable systems and technology beforehand that could either hinder friendly forces moving in or help remove support for opposing forces. The general targets of focus would be fields such as government, military, infrastructure, corporations/businesses that are friendly to the government, communications and so forth.

Considerations/Recommendations-

Unconventional forces fill in areas of operation that conventional forces are not quite created to fill. With this in mind, they USO's should be treated in an appropriate manner that is consistent with their duties in comparison to conventional forces. In general, conventional cyberwar operators will perform from a support standpoint whereas unconventional operators will be used in a more surgically targeted, offensive capacity. Emphasis will be on innovative tactics, attacking the enemy's technological infrastructure, sabotage and utilizing technical ability to protect ongoing operations behind enemy lines.

With continual striving that demands an innovative mind, increasing technological capability and street smarts, the USO will emerge a thorn in the side of any adversary or country who relies solely on technology.

Chapter 5: Counter-Guerilla Operations

Counter-Guerrilla: Guerilla warfare tends to be the predominant type of skirmishes that are currently occurring. Sometimes they are perpetrated by individuals involved in organized crime, other times by terrorists looking to cause serious harm to others or even extremist political hactivist groups who are willing to use dangerous measures to force political change. For the purposes of this book, we will bring together all separate groups under the banner of counter-guerrilla operations so as to discuss ways to better target groups who use technology and other methods of cyberwarfare to attack governments and the public.

Highly motivated, mobile teams are difficult to counter and require a healthy dose of patience to prosecute just as traditional counterinsurgency operations. Unlike conventional warfare, which prefers inversely more rigid tactics and strategies as well as defined opposing sides, guerrilla operations instead works towards utilizing very flexible tactics and strategies with a focus on making the most out of little. Tactics emphasize mobility, strong force multipliers and attacking centers of gravity with a premium placed on getting the most result with the least amount of resources.

Though typically this version of warfare is characterized by small groups of people who are fighting against a larger government in their own country, this can also be a term used for smaller groups in a foreign country who are helping or enabling others to conduct warfare against a much larger enemy. (Or in other cases, can be a small foreign group who is attempting to harass or cause problems for a much larger enemy.)

In cyberwarfare, the principles of guerilla related tactics still apply. It remains necessary to focus on hit and run attacks, staying hidden and overall focusing on a stealthy nature of operations when possible while emphasizing the balance between maximum impact in contrast to the relative cost/time needed. Strategy and tactics necessary for conducting successful harassment disproportionate to the group involved in cyberwar is for all intents and purposes the same as that utilized by traditional guerrilla tactics.

Those who are attempting to attack through technology will likely tend to rely on a few core principles that define what a guerilla fighter is: Anonymity, Mobility, and Innovative ability for example. These will form centers of gravity which are to be targeted so as to defeat the fighters. With a firmer understanding of what we are facing, we can begin developing strategy to combat this type of warfare.

> **Attack:** In general the desired aims of the group are what will determine the different attacks. Terrorists will seek to hit targets that will cause massive damage or gain considerable media news. Criminal organizations will move towards attacks that gain financial income while extremist hactivists will attempt to create media spectacles to force changes they feel need to be made in a political structure.

> With the understanding that such groups will be using guerilla type attacks, possible neutralization vectors can encompass many facets depending on the group that is involved.

We will start with a brief description of three general groups, namely that of terrorist and criminal organizations, then brainstorm some general ideas with which to act against them.

a. **Terrorist Organizations:** Many modern terrorist organizations tend to heavily rely on technology as it considerably enhances their logistical structure to a global scale, improves the ability to act, transmit messages and allows better coordination among other advantages.
   Terrorist organizations are those which tend to in particular use fear, threats of violence and death to support their operations and should receive a higher priority to neutralize vice criminals. (In particular if they are in the home country of a target.)

b. **Criminal Organizations:** Criminal organizations are usually wild cards in terms of how well they have adopted CW technology, if at all. The range of expertise varies wildly, from street gangs with no technological capability whatsoever beyond cell phones and social media accounts to highly organized criminal organizations that span the globe with former Special Operations troops among their ranks and advanced CW capability.

Unlike terrorist groups which should be persecuted with prejudice, a varying level of important can be given to a criminal organization depending on their aims, sophistication and capabilities.

Surveillance and Interception: Mass surveillance is already an oft used tool by most governments whenever possible. With the continued proliferation of advanced technology along with the continued improvement of ease of use, it is becoming easier and cheaper to monitor anyone, anywhere at any time. This can consist of multiple methods for tracking, including:

1) Tapping any form of communication, including telephonic voice calls, modems, fax, email, keystrokes, Internet communications, satellite voice, cellular voice and data along with VOIP conversations.

2) Mobile GPS trackers which can be attached to cars.

3) Automated software which keeps track of financial transactions while looking for anomalies.

These are powerful capabilities which can, and are already being used to disrupt both terrorist cells and criminal organizations. Examples include the ECHELON program, which enables the worldwide monitoring of commercial satellite trunk communications and the Stingray program, which allows for fake cellular towers to be created for surveillance, tracking and interception purposes. Because of the strength of such surveillance, when used, terrorists have occasionally opted to try and rely on technology as stealthily/with the smallest footprint possible while well-funded criminal organizations, such as the FARC have instead opted to take their technological capability to a significantly higher level.

Considering the strength of technological surveillance and interception capability, it becomes clear that the more advanced a country is on the CW scale, the greater likelihood that individuals or groups can be watched, tracked, and dismantled at will if there is any significant reliance on technology.

Powerful Decryption: Governments are increasingly struggling with military grade encryption which is available for all over the world, and even more so, for free. This includes data container protection programs, such as Pretty Good Privacy and Truecrypt, encrypted VOIP software, SSL for secure Internet communications and so forth. Naturally terrorist groups and criminal organizations have seized on this opportunity to give themselves some of the most secure communications that the underworld has ever seen. This has allowed for trustworthy communications and further increased efficiency of logistical operations as a result.

One particular case which made apparent just how strong and useful this encryption has shown itself was during the criminal trial of a man convicted of (drug?) offenses in South America. He was discovered to have a Truecrypt container and refused to give the password. The government was not able to penetrate into the container and discover its

131

contents despite collaborative efforts with the Federal Bureau of Investigation in the United States.

With this problem in mind, it becomes apparent that governments and militaries will need to focus on using different means to increase their capability at decrypting these types of communications so as to neutralize this feeling of general communication security and trustworthiness. There are current means already becoming available which provide a good start towards such decryption purposes, such as the use of GPU Cluster technology to replace CPU's to crack said passwords with multifold power at a much lower price than with general purposes supercomputers. Another option is to find mathematical weaknesses in the algorithm themselves used to encrypt information so as to break the code much faster. Of course this is becoming increasingly more difficult as the types of mathematical formulas being used become increasingly more difficult.

Use Law Enforcement (Local and International): Though this seems to be an obvious addition, however some would be surprised at the level to which law enforcement will not work with the government or military towards ridding their respective locales of criminal or terrorist influences. This comes down to old fashioned politics, bureaucratic spats and other non-electronic related reasons. Local law enforcement may refuse to work with government agencies simply because they believe it detracts from their own stature. (Or rationale that is even more base, such as simply because they do not like the people who are making the request.) International law enforcement may be even more difficult to work with depending on the politics of the situation. Regional, global, and personal interests will be particular factors to consider, though with some persuasion it may be possible to involve law enforcement in other countries as well. Emphasis on mutual gain, promise of political reward along with other political tools may prove helpful in this regard, depending on how far the host country/military is willing to go to confound/neutralize underground operators.

Co-Opt Internet Service Providers:
Attempting to co-opt ISP's to help look for underground operators can vary depending on their

relationship with the government in general. In some countries where the state has much more control over the media and Internet, compelling such companies can be much easier and thus more quickly root out problem elements. However in countries where there is more freedom of the press and less corruption, then there can be a corresponding difficulty in gaining the cooperation of service providers, unless it can be shown that an overriding national security concern is present.

However if cooperation can be obtained whether through persuasion or coercion then a tremendous tool will have fallen in the lap of those working to squelch underground operators. They will be able to tap Internet communications at will, see where they are communicating at, use their own Internet connection to hack the targets computer, install malicious software and essentially watch them with a microscope at will. Of course there will be downsides, such as not being able to watch encrypted traffic, however considering most of the world is currently still using the over decade old Windows XP operating system watching them may be easier than one would first suspect.

In essence, Internet Service Providers are the gatekeepers: Gaining their cooperation is important and will prove invaluable in neutralizing underground operations and operatives.

Considerations/Recommendations- No political system or government is perfect. There will always be members of the public at large who disagree with a particular policy, or a law and will go to varying lengths to show their displeasure. This has not changed in the Information Age, where instead of spray-painting graffiti on walls, people are not taking to defacing websites instead. Or instead of leaking information to news reporters, people are now taking to releasing embarrassing/damning information over the Internet. The people who commit such crimes should not be conflated with underground operatives (Such as terrorists or criminals) who are clearly in a different class and should be dealt with appropriately, such as utilizing local law enforcement.

Attempting to "throw the book" at such individuals who are venting their displeasure with the system only as having an unnecessarily heavy hand rather than real strength and should be viewed dimly unless necessary. Such a heavy handed approach makes the public wonder why the government is moving so hard against individuals who could be portrayed in a sympathetic light despite their crimes. (Many young individuals who are apart of hactivst groups for example, tend to be in their late teens to 20's.)

A similar type of strategy of "get them all" employed by the US based Motion Pictures Association was met with a severe public relations nightmare.[43] The MPAA could have made the case that there were individuals who were breaking the law and should be brought to justice. However rather than looking towards more unsympathetic targets such as the businesses who were trafficking in illegal software, they instead adopted a heavy handed, scorched earth campaign which perhaps caught some who had broken the law but also snared innocent grandmothers, pregnant women, teenagers, students and others who could barely afford school. (And were being slapped with life ruining, 6 figure damage awards by courts that the organization would

---

[43] Munslow, Amy. "RIAA Changes Strategy Deterring Illegal File Sharing." *The Michigan Daily*. N.p., 07 Jan. 2009. Web. 17 Feb. 2014.

obviously never be able to get from the defendant.) The result ended with some court victories but proved a devastating defeat in terms of public relations, to which the MPAA is viewed with considerable contempt to this day.

This real world example is a prime example which shows that counter-guerrilla tactics should not be used without restraint against everyday agitators. It should be focused where it belongs: Against more serious threats such as terrorists and criminal elements.

Chapter 6: Psychological Operations

Through Cybercorps specialists, cyberspace can stretched out beyond common attack and defense against technology into a more subtle strategy rooted in psychology, political warfare and encouraging an individual to change their mind through the power of mass media and technology. The field in using subtle and sometimes overt ways to influence the decision making of others is called PSYOP which stands for Psychological Operations. Nearly every country with an Internet connection already engages PSYOP to some degree online, however systematizing and creating doctrine towards the successful prosecution of warfare will enable a more effective campaign vice making decisions pell mell. (PSYOP material tends to lean towards the more conventional side and should be updated accordingly.)

Though the role of conventional PSYOP will continue to remain important as not every country heavily utilizes technology, however based on a world that is becoming more interconnected through the Internet, a single Cybercorp PSYOP specialist will find his ability to disseminate information to shape the will of another increased considerably in comparison to his conventional PSYOP counterpart. Though it is possible for conventional PSYOP to be applied anywhere in the world, the Cybercorp specialist has the ability to broadcast information globally at any location, anytime. A variety of methods can be employed to attempt and shape the will of others, including through online forums, news sites, attempted insertion of news in legitimate news networks, and so forth. The CSO will not subsume the role of traditional PSYOP specialists but rather act in concert with, and as a part of a team effort towards enhancing their ability.

PSYOP is a specialized field of which technical ability regarding technology/computers is not as important as regular ability, thus the CSO PSYOP specialist will be able to bring his technical capabilities to the table and increase PSYOP effectiveness. In the following sections we will discuss some of the strategic insights into how the CSO specialist can be help in PSYOP.

1. Global PSYOPS Abilities- The global nature of the Internet allows the CS specialist to strike anytime, in any country in the world. The attacker can further obfuscate and confuse by actually traveling inside said country and utilizing the same techniques so as not only allow plausible deniability by the host government but also give more creditability to the dissemination of said PSYOP as it is actually originating in the host country rather than through another.

Though the conventional operator may be limited based on geolocation, the PSYOP operator can utilize desktops, laptops, cellphones, harness social medial and a variety of other methods to operate virtually anywhere in the world with an impact which is incredibly disproportionate compared to the number of operators necessary. One lone operator can use desktops/laptops to operate in most major country, cell phone technology can be utilized through various dissemination methods such as texting, pirate radio and television broadcasts can be used or even attempting to hack news organizations of a host government to push out information which harasses the enemy, demoralizes the government, etc. The reach of the Cybercorps PSYOP specialist is only limited by the technological capability of their host country, the technological capability of the target country and their own ingenuity.

Plant false stories/Generate Rumors

aa. This method is mostly self-explanatory and would consist of using technological methods to disseminate misleading or completely false information for a variety of reasons, including demoralization and discrediting another. In general, the venue of dissemination would depend on the message being released, the type of PSYOP being conducted the aims of the host country/person. For example, white PSYOP would include creating websites that provide information through the Internet which consists of information that is true, verifiable and credible but subtly attempts to prefer releasing stories that are favorable to one group, or country while releasing negative facts regarding another. Countries in which cell phone usage is extremely prominent allows for another easy venue. Through text messaging, it is possible to systematically reach the vast majority of the country and spread a message of choice. Black PSYOP would use information that is barely true, false, or a subtle blend of truths with falsehoods so as to discredit, or at the least distract the person in a negative way.

Using the current system of differentiation between the levels of PSYOP used in conventional operations would also be prudent. Currently they are broken up between the white, grey and black levels with white being legitimate information sources that are slightly biased, to the grey which are not quite as trustworthy and give more blatantly biased information to black sources, which are sources set up for the sole purposes of spreading propaganda to a target audience.

Frighten Government Members

aa. Black PSYOP methods can be used in this level. Governments depend on politicians of different stripes to act as pillars and keep the government propped up. Without these pillars, the country could face collapse. Methods that can be used include disseminating false information to discredit effective politicians, providing information to prop up less effective or outright useless political figures or making anonymous threats to scare others out of office. Grey methods can also be used, including publicly posting information that is embarrassing to various political figures such as marriage infidelity, committing actions in direct opposition of publicly stated goals, involvement in crime and so forth. The aim of PSYOP mostly depends on the stated goals, white being used to support government figures who are at least sympathetic to the host nation, grey to include biased news reports attempting to accomplish the same to black, which involves direct attempts at discrediting, fear and moves to destabilize a group or government.

Frighten Military Leaders

aa. The mission focus remains the same as with government figures, however as per the namesake, this type of PSYOP instead moves against those in a countries military. Though it may be more difficult to conceive how it would be helpful to write bad news stories, spread rumors or other information could possibly hurt a military a leader, it is important to focus on the center of gravity that senior military officers, such as in the United States sit on: They may not require public support of any real variety, *however their bosses who choose to retain and promote them do.* One can rest assure that politicians are more than willing to cut ties, demote or outright remove competent military leaders who prove to be more political liability than they are worth.

This has happened many times in the past of the US Military in particular, such as when one of the foremost US Army Generals of the 21st century, former General David Petraeus was removed from his CIA Head posting due to allegations he had an illicit, ongoing affair.[44] Another example was former General Stanley McChrystal who was removed from his post while in the midst of making inroads during the counterinsurgency campaign in Afghanistan for making derogatory remarks about the presidential administration's handling of the war in Afghanistan in a popular magazine.[45]

Rumors, innuendoes and inferences are a powerful way to grease the skids of military officers who are otherwise very competent to be shoved out the door and replaced with far less effective officers.

---

[44] Dillon, Nancy. "Ex-CIA Director David Petraeus Apologizes for Affair in First Public Speech since Resignation ." *NY Daily News*. N.p., 26 Mar. 2013. Web. 17 Feb. 2014.
[45] Cooper, Helene, and David Sanger. "Obama Says Afghan Policy Won't Change After Dismissal." *New York Times*. N.p., 23 Jan. 2010. Web. 17 Feb. 2013.

In general there are far more military officers who are excellent at political intrigue and get to their position rather than competent officers who are skilled at warfare itself. Similar to attempts to coerce and change the will of politicians, a variety of methods can be used to attempt at a similar campaign against a host military as well. Like any military, there is a specific hierarchy and pillars of support which keep them strong. For some countries, pillars can be trust from the public, pride in their service and so forth. Cybercorp PSYOP attempts to disrupt this by attempting to discredit and embarrass military leaders, fomenting discontent in the military, using social media outlets to encourage the airing of grievances against said military, generate rumors that foster fear and dissension within the ranks or between the military and the public.

Frighten the Public

aa. Mass psychology is an interesting thing. There are many proven studies that show that even when people seem to know a fact, when surrounded by groups of people telling them otherwise, they will begin to doubt what they initially thought to be true.

Utilizing technology, one can foster PSYOP campaigns of incredible proportions to terrify, enrage or confuse the populace. The truth of what is going on with a situation is not as important as people *perceive* the situation to be. For example, there were firestorms of controversy during cases in the United States such as the 2013 trial surrounding Trayvon Martin and George Zimmerman. Though there may or may not have been a racial factor involved, there were a significant amount of people who regardless perceived a racial bias that was involved with almost no regards to the facts of the case or evidence that presented a contrary view. Soon after the case, there were multiple instances of civil disobedience from the west coast of the United States to the East coast, including blocking foot traffic in Times Square and putting a complete halt to a heavily trafficked Los Angeles freeway.[46] It is important for the PSYOP specialist to recognize this subtle undercurrent then press on it through varying types of news dissemination to a public. Finding the pillars of support that link a country to its people are the key,

---

[46] Blankstein, Andrew. "Trayvon Martin Protesters Block 10 Freeway in L.A." *Los Angeles Times*. Los Angeles Times, 14 July 2013. Web. 17 Feb. 2014.

though through the Internet the effects become massively disproportionate as compared to the amount of people affecting it.

Encourage the loss of Business

aa. In this case, we start with determining some of the causal factors involved in economic based decision making. When the public, businesses, governments or even banks make choices on what type of investments to get involved in, they make these choices based partly on knowledge and experience. However it is also the case is that there is an inherent level of psychological compulsion that will influence the inevitable decisions which are made.

Many factors can be involved in this psychological swaying of the mind, such as playing on a person's greed, fear, pride or even hatred. These base emotions, namely hatred was displayed in a visceral way in a public 2013 conflict between famed hedge fund managers Carl Icahn and Bill Ackman through a company named Herbalife. The conflict appears to have been instigated by Carl Icahn mostly due to bad blood over a prior bad business deal over a decade prior. In it, Bill Ackman was heavily shorting the company Herbalife, trying to put it out of business by claiming the business was a pyramid scheme. Carl Icahn went in with his own money, directly contradicting said story and possibly costing Ackman an enormous amount of money.[47]

In essence, as with other level of PSYOP we must first discover what type of outcome is desirable, (The downfall of a business, lowering stocks of publicly traded companies, the removal of competent economic managers, causing government related concerns and so forth) then study what centers of gravity must be targeted to achieve this outcome from a psychological standpoint. The damage that can be inflicted is almost incalculable, including using hacking based techniques to retrieve emails for blackmail purposes, publishing negative economic information via social media outlets, discovering and revealing personal embarrassing information on economic officials through either online discovery (Email, Chat, Social Media) or through surreptitious means. (Directly breaking into computer and installing keystroke loggers for example.) Hijacking mass media

[47] Vardi, Nathan. "Carl Icahn And Herbalife Are Crushing Bill Ackman." *Forbes*. Forbes Magazine, 21 May 2013. Web. 17 Feb. 2014.

outlet accounts, such as Twitter feeds and so forth allow for the possibility of creating instant mass media propagation and causing virtual instant crashes of targeted countries on stock exchanges. There are multiple methods available, however the main aim is to use all available cyberwar PSYOP techniques and create the necessary pressure/influence to compel another to do what is desired from an economic standpoint.

Of added interest is the ability to use the Internet to propagate information which can prop up or cause difficulties with another nation's finances. We begin by targeting the center of gravity for a nation's finances: Foreign investment and trust. Through prior mentioned techniques, we could for example begin instant, online news sources which appear for all intents and purposes to be legitimate outlets. However while releasing information that a typical news source would, there would be an emphasis on damaging data on the target country while making sure to ensure the widest dissemination. Such information, if it is picked up by reputable news outlets can prove damaging to governments attempting to bring in foreign investment or deter others from investing that otherwise might have. An example would be revelations that Apple was employing sweatshops in China to lower costs of production.[48] This provoked anger both in countries such as the United States, but also towards citizens of China itself who felt exploited. Though the information is true, it is necessary to either uncover the damaging information through varying means or to disseminate already available negative information as widely as possible. (Including through the Internet, social media, text messaging, etc.)

Considerations/Recommendations- The area of Psychological Operations has been used to deadly effect throughout virtually all of recorded history. One particularly effective, conventional operation was used during in World War II, name Operation Fortitude. The Allied Forces desired to invade Normandy and begin an assault against Axis forces, however leadership at the time was fearful of the possible causality numbers they would, thus Operation Fortitude was created to convince the Axis that the Allies would attack Pas Del

---

[48] Cooper, Rob. "Inside Apple's Chinese 'sweatshop' Factory Where Workers Are Paid Just £1.12 per Hour to Produce IPhones and IPads for the West." *Mail Online*. Associated Newspapers, 25 Jan. 2013. Web. 17 Feb. 2014.

Calais rather than Normandy. They created an entirely fictional Army group led by General Patton, with fake tanks, encampments, military units, radio signals and even false reports sent from captured German spies which convinced important German leaders to shift their forces away from Normandy. The invasion was spectacularly successful.

Much effort was put into Operation Fortitude and the gamble paid off handsomely. To this day, traditional PSYOP continues to be a powerful weapon in the toolbag of any country and will be not be departing completely in a traditional sense anytime soon. However nimble, global communication systems, the Internet and simple technology can offer a powerful amplifying effect on traditional psychological warfare which will make USO's capable of achieve much more in in comparison to traditional methods with less inherent effort.

Chapter 7: Intelligence

Intelligence is the cornerstone of many government institutions, including law enforcement, military and overseas agencies. Through it, one can used trained agents that will go and seek out opportunities to sift and gain knowledge through a variety of means, including electronics, other people and data analysis. As knowledge is power, harnessing the latest methods to develop an arsenal of influence will continue to be of great importance. The latest and still developing field of intelligence will be through computer, Internet and technological based means. Personnel trained in technological warfare or at a minimum, given a greater understanding of the capabilities of, and how an opposing countries technology can affect them will continue to be of primary importance as we see computers evolve.

To this end, we will be looking to new units called Espionage Specialists who will be specifically trained technological specialists that will use their talents to engage in low and hi-tech espionage. In this capacity they will fulfill an unconventional role by infiltrating into various target countries with the specific purpose of attempting to spy from inside the host country. There are a variety of ways that the Cybercorps specialist can stand in this role, such as installing keyloggers onto computers, giving away USB related drives which include command and control software/malware, installing software which monitors mouse movement, takes screenshots and captures audio or video feed from the hosts computer, surreptitious audio and video capture of targets via cellphone, utilizing phone cloning to listen in on phone calls or even installing malware into a cell phone, computer or mobile device that can be connected through remotely so as to gain information on what the target is doing. (This does not necessarily have to be only the Internet: Any technology that radiates electromagnetic pulses can be captured and tapped into. This includes RF, Light waves, Microwave and so forth.) It is very difficult in light of the newly dawning Information Age for adversaries to conduct activities with absolutely no technology whatsoever. (Though able to stay hidden for over a decade, even the infamous Osama Bin Laden was discovered to possess a laptop with Internet connection and a TV. He was also rumored to pay close attention to the news as well.) The focus of the Unconventional

Espionage Cybercorp agent is gaining intelligence through any technological means possible.

1) Collection Operations:

a. Traditional HUMINT (Human Intelligence) operators remain irreplaceable in gaining on ground knowledge; however there is also something to be said for the ripe opportunity to take advantage of specifically trained hackers who are deployed out of country to engage in collection operations. In this capacity they will fulfill a covert role by infiltrating into various target countries with the purpose of using a wide variety of technological means to gain information and data on the target. The desired outcome of these types of operations will not be attempting to interpret the data, but rather seeking to answer questions that are proposed by the supporting government. Examples of such particular knowledge that could be provided in support of intelligence requirements could be to map all wireless access points within a given area, hacking into encrypted wireless routers to record all information that passes through it, tapping fiber optic lines, tapping major telephone trunks, installing software in databases to track economic activity, installing hardware/software based keyloggers onto computers, giving away USB related drives which include command and control software, installing software which monitors mouse movement, takes screenshots and captures audio or video feed from the hosts computer, etc.

As we can see there is a tremendous amount of data that can be gathered, however there is the additional bonus that as this information is being acquired from inside the target country itself it is much more difficult to pinpoint who is responsible. Further, in many cases it is difficult to even pinpoint that any information as actually stolen in the first place, must less tracking down the perpetrators that were involved in said operations.

2) Online Infiltration: Public venues offer a wealth of information as to what is going on throughout particular communities. Many times, by simply hanging out at certain cafés, bars, and other such venues one can ascertain general feeling regarding certain events in a country. Further, one can also gain valuable information by gaining access to the haunts of particular groups or people that one wishes to learn more about.

These same principles can also be applied towards espionage online. There are a multitude of online forums that are used for public discourse in various countries around the globe. They can be useful for gauging public sentiment, or paying attention for the inadvertent release of sensitive information. (People can have just as big of mouths online as they can in person, sometimes even more so due the somewhat anonymous nature of forum posts.) This can be via places such as video websites, public and specialty forums, or social media. Other places can include online video games with text-based chat, audio coordination servers for video games, and private forums. (Such as those on the TOR based Darknet.) Though finding private places for conversation will be much more lucrative in terms of information, however often one can find interesting nuggets of information in public discourse as a surprising amount of people with some level of public influence post more often online than ever before.

The old psychological adage remains the same online as well as offline: People love to talk. Those who possess this mentality and meaningful information should be watched and tracked when possible.

3) Upgrade Current Operations: Many of the benefits that can be afforded to Special Operation personnel through technological upgrades can also prove helpful to those involved in collection operations abroad. The focus should be either in giving necessary knowledge to better improve the skills of current officers, or by giving easy to use devices that enhance the abilities of officers in the field. This can include military-grade encryption software, encrypted voice/chat, online dead-drop areas, online money laundering, basic online PSYOP capabilities and so forth.

When speaking in regards to "necessary knowledge" , we should also become acquainted with what exactly "necessary" is. The problem with defining such a term lies in the slippery nature of technology itself: It is growing at such an exponential rate that even today, our current technological state is light years beyond just 5 or so years ago. Rather than setting absolute standards, having a more fluid benchmark of general understanding that can be built on along with a corresponding specialty would be helpful. For example, a short lesson involving a practical exercise to demonstrate computer/electronic basics would be helpful. In such a class the students would gain an understanding of how current computers work, how to manipulate software for various ends and use them as force enhancement tools.

After learning from a basic core of knowledge with which to build on, a field should be chosen to specialize in, such as using software-based encryption or setting up basic systems to defeat electromagnetic communications. Though the term "specialize" is being used, in reality expectations should be managed carefully: Training in such an area should be given with the understanding that the student likely has a certain level of technical expertise, (Quite possibly none at all) and is being trained in the absolute basics necessary to enhance his ability to successfully leverage technology towards achieving intelligence goals.

4) Counterterrorism

a. Counter-terror efforts will focus on using technology available and devising further innovations for the purpose of either finding terrorist elements overseas and/or shutting down the technology that they may rely on. Though one could offer the argument that most terrorists do not rely on technology as much as before due many concerns of being tracked, however just as with major countries, the convenience and staggering effectiveness/efficiency that it offers makes technology simply too attractive to completely give up. Because of this, technology can be considerably useful in tracking terrorist and curtailing their operations.

Besides the helpfulness from a stationary standpoint, I would also envision corollary elements being set up to prepare for the future of counter-terror operations. This would include highly mobile, technically sophisticated units or groups who strive to stay hidden, strike quickly and then fade into the shadows. CT Cyber efforts will focus on creating honeypots, monitoring websites, using various triangulation technology for tracking purposes, (GPS, cell phone, iPad's, computers, wireless, etc.) using software and hardware to disrupt terrorist related operations and so forth. Of further help would be using various schemes to track terrorists, such as finding surreptitious ways to give them tech which can be monitored (Cell phones, Tablets, Laptops), or bugging technology that they already own. (Through software such as keylogging software, or hardware which conducts packet capturing/keylogging operations.) Certain computer screens can even be monitored from a distance with hardware which enables operators to remotely recreate the radiation emanating from CRT screens, thus watching exactly what the person is doing.

Terrorist elements which do operate in a completely technophobic vacuum still give themselves way in another sense: Throughout most of the world, virtually all people use some type of technology, whether it be TV's, cellphones, radios or any other manner of communication. If there are areas that heavily use television, the Internet or other forms of communication, then by the very nature of the fact that there are sections in which *no one* is using any form of technology could be considered valuable places to look.

Considerations/Recommendations- Intelligence agencies tend to break up their departments based on specialty. Typically divisions of specialty range from technology, to human intelligence or imagery. However this creates somewhat a disconnect that should be addressed, namely core collectors who have excellent people skills but have not received adequate training in technology. With basic training in low to zero cost software and technology, along with some basic innovative skills, a much more effective officer will be produced.

In short, the benefits of having good, basic fundamental knowledge of technology and how to manipulate it towards intelligence requirements far outweighs simply allowing people to proceed as though a technological revolution is not occurring as we speak. Short of complete country-wide surveillance, such as that of countries like North Korea, the benefits can be staggering in comparison to the risk.

Though there tends to be state efforts at controlling the information from time to time, such as in the United States, China and Russia, however there are simply too many types of software that can help facilitate communications, financial support and other activities, many without even requiring an Internet connection. (Though this would make the tasks considerably easier.) Short of either a complete clampdown of the country or shutting down the Internet itself, it simply is neither feasible nor possible at this time to stop such software/hardware beyond temporary closures.

One of the greatest strengths of such an approach lies in the fact that unlike the bulk of counterterror forces which tend to remain in a host country, these tactical, mobile teams will be sent around the world covertly to conduct operations as necessary and can be considerably difficult to track by technological means.

Chapter 8: Current Threats

Current lay of the Land- Who the major players are and what is occurring in the field of technological security is continually dynamic and fluid. Virtually any government with the resources is straining to gain as much advantages as possible through computers, while smaller groups with different political agendas are also attempting to use technology for their own ends. As it stands, there appears to be 4 main types of actors on the stage: Governments, who are leveraging technology to spy on their own people/others while accusing others of doing the same, the military of whom are working unceasingly towards trying to modernize their forces and meet government requirements, subversive groups who are moving to amplify their capabilities beyond what was possible in the past and finally, law enforcement.

Law enforcement, in countries such as in the United States are taking advantage of largely antiquated laws to spy on, keep databases of and track virtually any person in the country. Many times these searches, spying and so forth are covered up with the soft blanket of "protecting the public" from terrorists, child molesters, or some other publicly maligned individual to essentially justify any and all actions by law enforcement.

These are the main actors that should be given the most time and consideration. The thought process upon how to utilize or defeat such a force would be mostly based on which side is advocating such warfare and who we are looking to defend against. Governments could struggle with law enforcement that has gained too much power, or in some countries it may be the military struggling against an oppressive regime that clings to power.

After establishing a cyber-force, a "Lay of the Land" should be developed. This method of studying will involve creating a visual representation of the different players in the field of cyberwar, who needs to be focused on and finally, a list of strengths, weaknesses and possibilities for exploitation. Besides the above major players as listed above, in this chapter we will list some more possible individuals or groups that can also be identified that one may have to contend with as well.

Lone Wolves:

Terrorists- Terrorist groups have come full force into the technological age with shocking speed. Al-Qaeda has been a prominent example of this, using technology as a heavy force multiplier to create one of the first, loosely connected, world-wide terrorist groups who used the Internet to keep in touch. Because of the heavy need for a terrorists attack to be disproportional to the actual amount of effort/man hours used, we can conclude that the future terrorist will continue to rely more on technology as the years go on. Of further concern is the fact that as terrorists become more adept at utilizing technology to achieve their goals, other nations are also becoming more dependent on our system of technology thus becoming more vulnerable to these sorts of attacks. Many of the same tactics that guerrilla fighters use will be directly applicable to terrorist individuals and groups as well. Methods of encryption, communication, financial movement and so forth will all prove to be potent force multipliers to the terrorist group.

Force multipliers are powerful with terrorists, for example the use of bitcoin to shift around funds without fear of arousing suspicion through money laundering controls in financial institutions, governments or other groups. In essence, it is possible for a man to take millions of dollars and send it via email, USB or even via floppy drive to transport to other countries. This revolutionary technology can be used to funnel funds from any country in the world so as to make operations more efficient.

Another example is encryption software, which facilitates and adds a layer of security to communications. Many of these types of software are freely available on the Internet and well known for their extreme difficulty in cracking. Such software can include VOIP software for audio/voice, PGP for whole disk encryption (thus preventing access to even booting up the computer) or other such software, such as Truecrypt. Truecrypt allows one to create encrypted "containers" which can be filled with various levels of information that one does not want another to get their hands on.

Another technology which will prove helpful to terrorists involves the ability to rapidly move information through mediums which for the most are surreptitious and difficult to monitor. Examples include software such as Bittorrent. Through this software, one can create a "torrent" file which maps files to be downloaded, then when a person downloads the torrent file can immediately begin downloading the file from all connected sources. Thus one could create an encrypted container then leave it at home while only bringing a copy of the torrent file, effectively creating a digital dead box so as to download it from anywhere in the world. This leaves little trace for anyone to find beyond short Internet transactions and of course the possibility that the tracker file itself may be retrieved.

Defeaters- The individual terrorist/group is difficult to move against by technological methods. A variety of methods can be used to blunt or defeat the terrorist however.

1. Honeypots- Honeypots are baited traps that are set up by computer experts. They are created with the intention of presenting a relatively easy target to hack with fake information that appears important. Instead of stopping the hacker, honeypots will instead log their tactics, location and what information they are trying to access. This is a powerful tool for discovering who the attacks are, where they are

attacking from, and more importantly gaining a better sense if there is foreign government involvement.

2. Interception of communications- Surveillance has been well discussed in this book and will be instrumental in capturing attackers. (Usually when invoking terrorism it tends to be much easier to garner support for further surveillance, Stingray trackers etc.)

3. Keystroke loggers- There are hardware and software based models available that can be used to capture every keystroke made by a particular person. This can prove beneficial in particular towards people or groups who are security conscious and use strong encryption. One can simply install a keylogger, wait for them to type the password and save years of trying to decrypt it through brute forcing.

4. Searching for, infiltrating and logging bittorrent swarms-Bittorrent swarms are excellent avenues for dead boxes for individuals to collect information as needed. For example, a bitcoin wallet could be seeded while the individual is given a coded torrent file to use. When needing to obtain the digital currency, he/she only needs to open the torrent file

and can download the file instantaneously from anywhere in the country. Surveillance and logging capabilities can be employed to break up such activity or at the least, keep tabs on what is going on.

5. Attempting to trace/crack digital currency transactions- This is more difficult to conduct at this time, but not impossible. For bitcoin in particular, the 51% problem[49] is still one of the kinks that the core developers are still trying to work out. Digital tumblers also make tracing the movement of bitcoin more difficult, however again this is a field that needs to be better pursued.

Attempting to find and defeat a foe adept at hiding can frustrating. This was seen in particular when the United States was fighting Al-Qaeda and associated terrorist groups in the wars of Afghanistan and Iraq. Their strength lies in fear, speed and an absolute necessity to constantly innovate or be overpowered by a stronger enemy. However the terrorist faces one problem: There are far fewer of them, with far fewer resources than a government

---

[49] Liu, Alec. "Bitcoin's Fatal Flaw Was Nearly Exposed." *Motherboard*. N.p., 10 Jan. 2014. Web. 17 Feb. 2014.

could muster. Though there may be some who are particularly intelligent and able to innovate consistently and effectively, if a country of a significant size (For example the United States, which has over 310 million people as of this writing) were to begin effectively searching for talent which prove exceptional at off-the-cuff thinking, they will strongly counter any such innovations quickly and effectively themselves.

Hactivists- Hactivists are groups of politically minded hackers (or in some cases, script kiddies) who use various methods to raise awareness of a political issue. These methods are usually related to different attention gathering measures, such as defacing a website, DoSing servers or in some cases, real life measures such as altering signs or TV's to display a message. However for the most part, Hactivists are harmless, though people do tend to get embarrassed if the issue they are trying to bring attention to is politically sensitive.

Defeaters- Though they are attempting to bring attention to an issue, I would suggest 2 considerations to be brought forward when such events occur:

1) Is the issue really a matter of security or a serious crime, or is this just a matter of someone being embarrassed? It is important to remember that we are discussing cyberwarfare. Events occur, such as those propagated by hactivists that may embarrass some, especially politicians or corporations, but does the response really warrant the utilization of cyberwarfare in response? The answer to that question is no. There are two reasons why this is a bad idea:

a) It plays directly into the hands of the hactivst: It gives them the attention they desire, and/or it brings attention to the issue they are trying to force attention onto.

b) It unnecessarily raises the ire of hacker communities worldwide. When a hacker group such as Anonymous defaces a website to bring attention to for example, a human rights issue, then it is only a small measure to simply restore the site from backups. Though one could vigorously pursue a case and attempt to put said hackers in jail, it is not only not particularly worth the time, but the relatively guaranteed bad public relations issues after when attempting to defend putting 17 year old hackers in jail isn't exactly great for any ones reputation. Not only that, but it makes said hacked site look even more foolish because they weren't hacked by some mysterious mastermind hacker that the public believes pulled it off, but instead a mere young teenager armed with a little knowledge and some utility he likely found off the Internet. Nonsense like people demanding the death of a political figure on Twitter or vociferously arguing over some inflammatory topic on Facebook is better just left alone. It makes the prosecuting government/company just look petty. (Even rock bands can't get away with this: The famous rock band, "Metallica" is still looked at derisively over a decade later for attempting to shut down Napster. Their image as a rich rock band who was out of touch with its fan base was particularly noteworthy.)

2) If the issue is serious enough, for example credible threats of violence or crimes such as attacking hospitals or police stations. These are indeed serious and should be pursued with all

deliberate speed. I would recommend releasing little public information until the perpetrator is caught. When he is caught, attempt to use the event to praise members of the CW team involved in catching him and also to bring prestige on the Cybercorps organization itself. The more dangerous the hack the better, because the hacker community thrives on individual reputation: If catching a particular hactivist was notoriously hard, then publicly rewarding the individuals for such an effort will prove very fruitful. Not only will it enhance the individuals reputation, of who can go and attract others in the hacking community, but also the institution itself which is paramount.

In summary, hactivists can be annoying but are best left ignored in terms of cyberwarfare. The benefit usually isn't worth the effort and bad public relations. (If not with the public, than with the hacking community itself.) Give due consideration, decide if it is a serious crime (without consideration for political embarrassment) then move on. Though some manager may think the political gain from helping a figure will make the hunt acceptable, however they ignore the fact that that increasing hacker knowledge

is cheap: Loss of reputation through serving political ends will simply destroy what the institution is trying to accomplish.

Individual Hackers

Defeaters- This section should be started with a caveat: Skilled individual hackers, within reason, should be the focus of recruiting measures rather than attempting to put away in prison. Naturally the desire for recruiting skilled individuals should be counter-weighted against other mitigating factors, such as criminal background, trustworthiness, and so forth however the initial question should be this: Based on the potential value of this person's skill, how strongly does it weigh against possible criminal issues? Very likely, the crimes committed appear alarming on its face but in reality are not particularly worrisome or in some cases, are clearly juvenile and not particularly dangerous except for embarrassing people.

1. With that said, we move on to individuals. It is important to remember what exactly a hacker is, vice the popular understanding of the name in the public sphere.

The large majority of people labeled "hackers" have little to no ability whatsoever. The majority are more appropriately labeled, "Script Kiddies." (Further discussion about script kiddies will be discussed later in this chapter.) A script kiddie is the derisive term used for people who discover automated tools, or semi-automated tools with little user interaction and generally have little talent. To emphasize, /these are not hackers./ They are also not the type of people that should be considered for future recruitment and in particular should be noted as a nuisance. Many of the cyberattacks that have been seen worldwide were generally done on Windows based computers, with Windows based utilities that the individual was taught how to use. China is particularly notorious for this type of hacking, as the majority of the world still uses Windows-based computers and thus, are still vulnerable to many of these types of attacks. Though "hacking attacks" can be frightening, what is more important is the sophistication of the attacks such as Stuxnet and Flame. For example, if every computer in the world shifted their operating system from Windows to Linux, then the Chinese threat would be considerably blunted. Consider the culture of said nations as well: The Americans tend to focus on an innovative spirit which is essential to hacking. Cultures that focus on mechanical thinking tend to struggle in hacking, because the very field of hacking itself demands innovation and thinking outside of the box.

The first and only true category of hacker are those who use their skills to exploit technology in a fashion that it was originally unintended for. In general, the public sphere views hacking as an exclusively computer based activity. (In particular view software.) However the more knowledgeable in the computer community disregards this, instead adhering to the original user of the term. Hacking can involve anything with a technological bent, including houses, cars, cell phones, iPad's and so forth. These are the people that need to be aggressively studied and recruited. The strength of an individual hacker's talent lies not only in an almost obsessive desire for knowledge and mechanical ability, but also in an innovative spirit that is difficult to cultivate. These type of talents are those which must be recruited. Bringing in people with computer talent enhances the prestige of the organization that manages to acquire them and if treated well will likely suggest friends of theirs to be apart of the same organization.

2. If the individual cannot or will not join the Cybercorps organization, then the real work begins:

a) Is the individual a threat? - Or to better phrase, is this a person a script kiddie who is merely being a nuisance or a real threat?

b) Is he a threat because he really is a threat or because another individual/corporation/government felt embarrassed and put a bulls eye on him?

c) Where is the individual located? - For domestic concerns, it is better to assist local authorities in discovering the identity of the individual/collecting evidence, but allowing local authorities to deal with the matter from a legal standpoint. (ie, let them have the evidence, arrest the individual and in general act only in a assistance related way.) For foreign concerns:

1) Develop a dossier- Who is this guy? What country does he reside in? Is it an allied or enemy country? Is he alone, a part of a group, corporation, gang, or state-sponsored cyberwarfare group? What

are his skills? Does he have a reputation in the hacking or computer/electronic security community?

2) Work with foreign governments first- If the person is simply a nuisance, assist and work with foreign governments and provide evidence leading to the arrest of the individual.

3) If this isn't possible, is utilizing cyberwarfare the best option?

4) If working with a foreign government isn't possible and the individual is a considerable threat, then real world solutions should be considered, including blunting his attacks through software developed by the host nation, destroying his computer through remote attacks or in extreme cases, elimination.

Considering the likely strong benefits that would be gained from recruiting an individual who has seemed to have gained notice by a government or country wide police force, then it is most prudent to attempt to gain the allegiance of the individual by any means necessary, while resorting to more forceful methods as a last resort.

Script Kiddies- Script kiddie is a term used in the hacking and computer community in general with great derision. As mentioned earlier, it is an individual who has little to no skills whatsoever. They are adept at running programs that others have created and tend to manipulate the lack of computer knowledge of others to present the image of being a hacker. A knowledgeable computer user can however quickly discern whether the person actually possesses any level of skill.

Defeaters- Law enforcement is the best way to deal with this problem. Though it may be helpful to utilize Cybercorps elements to aid law enforcement, again law enforcement should be the weapon of choice for dealing with such an individual.

1. If law enforcement is not a possibility and such a script kiddie possesses particularly powerful tools, such as large DDoS botnets, etc., then there are likely 2 ways to best go about it:

a) Use skilled hackers to analyze the code being used and defeat it if possible.

b) Attempt to find and directly attack the user's computer

c) Attempt to attack the group: In cases of countries who decide to use script kiddie type attacks, such as automated Windows tools, then it is possible to attack the systems themselves. If they have an Internet connection and are conducting attacks, then they are simultaneously vulnerable to attacks. One needn't look further than IP logs and conduct some simple detective work to figure which country the attacks are arriving from.

Groups with Technological Prowess

Hacker Groups- Hacking groups are the most difficult for a country to deal with. They are technologically sophisticated groups of individuals generally, have high levels of talent, innovation and are becoming increasingly aware of the desire for their talents. (Along with the growing realization that there is a serious shortage of their talents.) A hacking group, depending on their level of sophistication can be difficult to deal with, but more troubling is nation-state who hire hacking groups to fight for them via proxy.

Defeaters

a. Can't beat em, join em: This strategy entails the likely easiest way to defeat a hacking group. One way to go about this would be to create a prestigious program that attracts talent and strongly sloughs off politics. All too often people with little to no talent whatsoever are put in charge of managing groups of hackers and thus if there ever was prestige in the first place, it is quickly lost. If a program is started that is well known for only attracting and retaining the best, then as the prestige grows then people will naturally gravitate towards joining. Do people join the Navy SEALS, Delta Force, or the CIA for the money? Of course not.

Criminal Organizations- Groups of individuals such as grey hat hackers and hacktivists generally do so for reasons that are non-financial in nature. Criminal organizations however are almost squarely focused on the acquisition of money and improving operations through the use of computers and advancement in technology. And as of this writing, they have done exceptionally well. Groups such as the Cartels in Mexico have made great use of simple, effective communications technology to avoid government detection. Criminal organizations in South America have put to use publicly available and free encryption software to protect their databases from discovery by law enforcement, while groups in Eastern Europe consistently attempt to fraudulently take money from financial institutions or in many cases, outright break into and rob the banks themselves online. The frontier of criminal enterprises has changed radically, with even the most basic street gangs now using online social media, email and cell phones to coordinate criminal activity. Complex criminal organizations that are on the proverbial map of the police and law enforcement must continue to innovate to stay alive, thus the government/law enforcement must also emphasize such a process to stay ahead of the game.

How can one go about stemming the tidal wave of criminal organizations that are virtually light years ahead of law enforcement in terms of adaptation of technology?

The first would be targeting the individuals who are providing expertise to such organizations. This can range from hobbyists with a good fundamental understanding of tech to military trained communicators with special operations training. In general, the motivation for getting involved in such work is simply for money. In general, communications, computers and technology can seem like an easy field to get involved with, even with criminal organizations, because there is no blood being spilled in the persons face. They can silently work in their workshops doing what they are already doing and make much more money than they ever would with government or other organizations.

With this in mind, we would begin looking to how to work and mitigate the flow of highly specialized help to them. As the focus will mostly be financial, attempts should be made to counterbalance the desire for financial incentives with either deterrents (Prison, ostracized from society, fines), attempts to lure them away (Offer legitimate jobs for them to do what they love legally) or more coercive methods if necessary. Though there are some who do provide highly technical services for other reasons, such as they have been perhaps blackmailed, or people they care about are being threatened, in general the rationale is illegally making as much money as possible.

Finally, after individuals the technology itself should be targeted. Though there are cases where some of the most well financed of criminals will be able to acquire up to military grade and other hi-tech tools, the general focus should be on the use of low-tech ways of gaining easier, less noticeable advantages. For example, why steal military grade encryption gear when you can simply download a free, publicly available toolkit? (Or at most, pay a small fee for the software.)

The real challenge will be moving after consumer grade software and hardware that offers capabilities that are leaps and bounds above government capabilities. What could be considered one of the defining strengths of certain governments, such as that of the United States, is the fact that the pace for moving legislation is generally slow. This is effective, so as to allow gradual change over time, but prevent certain people from being elected into office and radically changing everything with unchecked authority. However there is a weakness to this that is correlated strongly with the technological arms race: Technology is changing so rapidly that it has quickly outpaced government change to keep certain elements in check. Without a streamlined ability to defeat certain dangerous technology while investigating criminal enterprises, governments and law enforcement will find it increasingly difficult to catch and put away such people.

Unfortunately targeting the tech itself can be fraught with ethical implications and concerns. If a government is ethically constrained and unwilling to target software, then obviously this method of mitigating technology towards criminals will be hampered, but not impossible. (Though in cases of law enforcement offices with little funding will find it much more difficult to counter.) Those who are ethically constrained will have to focus on legal measures to stop the flow of such tech. This can include working closely with private industry partners that are willing to create backdoors in their software and hardware, tagging hardware with AGPS/GPS trackers, installing keyloggers onto computer systems, or being given legal permission by judicial officials to conduct certain activities.

Without legal or ethical constraints, the government can be considerably deadly when moving against criminal organizations technical ability. This can include infecting the BIOS/Operating Systems of different pieces of technology while still being built in factories, intercepting communications traffic through the air, intercepting technology shipments (including via regional and local carriers) to infect systems or even purposefully rigging industrial grade technology to suffer catastrophic failures after a period of time. Without ethical constraints, a complex criminal organizations ability to use technology can be quite hampered, however it should be noted that the ethical problems inherent with such approaches could be more dangerous to the government employing them than the activity itself.

In general, combatting criminal organizations should be left to law enforcement. Only in the rare case that an organization has become so powerful that they are able to challenge the government itself should the decision be considered to move in military cybercorps troops to begin targeting their operations. (Though this would not preclude using cybercorps troops as advisors/putting them under the temporary command of law enforcement to aid in operations.)

Terrorist Organizations- The term "terrorist" has been floating around recent years much more than past years. The 9/11 attacks along with the subsequent "War on Terror" that the United States has been pursuing around the globe has indelibly impressed the image and ideas of what one is on the American consciousness. However when pressed, what exactly a "terrorist" is tends to prove pretty elusive. For the purposes of this section, knowing what exactly a terrorist is as compared to the term freedom fighter will not be addressed. Whether labeled terrorist, freedom fighter or some other term, what is of more concern is the tactics being used and how to defeat them regardless of that opponent's label.

In general, groups using guerrilla tactics have managed to take good advantage of the technological revolution to support their purposes. Of course it doesn't hurt that in the past, constant innovation is necessary for their group to thrive. They have largely adopted technology in the way that many governments are still struggling to do, or simply have not done so at all.

Examples of new frontiers for terrorists is replete, with virtually every new copy of "Popular Science" magazine proving to be a staggering cornucopia of reports on cutting edge/game changing technology that can be set up in a dual use capacity. Two particular relatively new systems that have been discussed recently are miniaturized UAV's/drone technology[50] and new CubeSat's.

After the debut of the Predator and Reaper drones, especially with the addition of offensive weapons such as missiles, we have seen a skyrocketing in interest as the technological know-how necessary for such equipment has become more user friendly and cheaper. It has become so easy to use that recently in the United States, animal activist group PETA were taken to court over their use of drone technology, ostensibly to track hunters who were tracking animals. Of recent days, a handheld drone was recently released that weighed barely over

[50] Piore, Adam. "Rise Of The Insect Drones." *Popular Science*. N.p., 29 Jan. 2014. Web. 17 Feb. 2014.

2 pounds with an almost 30 minute battery life that could act in a reconnaissance capacity. Though we are now seeing a reaction from the military in regards to such systems, such as the Navy and Air Force's improved lasers that specifically target drones, there should still be concern that such drones are becoming so ubiquities and smaller.

Satellite technology and launching vehicles are also now accessible for the average group, such as through CubeSat's that are audio/video capable and can also relay data signals. CubeSat's are small to miniaturized satellites that can be sent into space and provide very limited capabilities, such as relaying data or audio. They are mostly used for amateurs and universities so as to learn more about satellite technology and sometimes just for fun. However there should also be concern, as a strong capacity isn't necessary for terrorist groups to launch their own satellites into space (If they haven't already) so as to provide surprised capabilities that are unexpected. Though it is understandable that anti-satellite weapons are also being sought to be banned from some countries, however a limited capability should still be developed to defeat such technology in the future.

One of the strengths of terrorist groups that governments generally struggle to match is the fact that terrorists are nimble in adopting new innovations that can improve their ability to field operations, while governments are usually slow and staggering giants. It will be difficult as there are always elements of politics that are involved, along with the possibility of interference from military leaders who also, traditionally desire a certain status quo; however there must be a focused effort on developing streamlined processes to bring in and field new innovations to combat these game changers.

An excellent example of such a process that other organizations should consider emulating would be programs like DARPA. Though it isn't necessary to have the greatest minds or the greatest budget, what matters most is getting such a project off the ground, sifting for the most innovative minds available and making at least a token effort to begin stemming the tide in the host countries favor. (Note: DARPA possesses a mere 140 technical specialists in a country with a population of over 300 million!)

Considerations/Recommendations- The vast majority of books written have a shelf life or lifeline in which the information pertaining to a field remains relevant. Very few become timeless classics that survive the test of history and still impart practical knowledge that remains relevant, such as Carl von Clausewitz "On War" or Sun Tzu's "On War." As with any level of warfare however, it is important to know who the players are and what you are dealing with in any given arena. Just as certain hackers, terrorist groups and governments have gained strength by leaps and bounds since the beginning of the Information Era, more individuals with different names and capabilities will continue to emerge and move to exert influence and power. Watching the field as it expands and evolves, while annotating the different strengths and weaknesses of future allies and enemies will of course remain paramount.

One particular recommendation that could prove to be useful would be developing global threat maps for visualizing threats. This would be a relatively generic world map, such as what Google Earth offers that lists different threats depending on the supposed country of origin, along with links to classified networks that can provide extra information mined from intelligence sources (HUMINT, MASINT, etc) and give a better picture of each group. Having basic wiki-style pages that discuss the group in further detail based on classification level could also give military planners and policymakers the ability to make more informed decisions.

Chapter 9: Forecasts for future threats

So far we have taken a look into the history of cyberwar, advocated the creation of a new agency that deals exclusively in technology-based warfare and also considered applications and modifications to the various spectrums of warfare. In this chapter we will spend some time exploring the future of this field, upcoming technologies and possible future threats to consider.

One of the exciting and perhaps frightening aspects of this rapidly evolving type of warfare is how literally an entirely new paradigm shift has evolved in such a rapid time over the last few years. As far as back the 1990's, varying attempts have been made to utilize modern technology and computers to cause damage to other businesses, engage in theft, espionage from other governments and so forth. However it is over roughly the last decade that we have seen an explosion in the complexity of newer attacks and more importantly, how much damage they can really cause. This considerable increase in power over the last fears can partly be attributed to the innovative ability of newer programmers, those who have become good at disruptive thinking and so forth, however the real common denominator appears to be the increasing reliance that the world has on technology.

Virtually anything that is commonly used in this current age has some form of CPU chip that is attempting to make things more efficient. It has become worrying to an extent, because older technology such as the landline telephone and mail are being kicked to the curb. Of course it is harder to justify keeping such older methods of information transport alive, however if for example by accident or design the electromagnetic spectrum was compromised, or perhaps the Internet was suddenly irreversibly shut down, then everything would come to a screeching halt. It is much easier to knock over cell phone towers than to cut landline telephone cables. (Even worse, assuming that the cell phone towers are able to stay up, if you lose power to your phone then you are out of luck, unlike with a landline.)

The future applications of newer gadgets and ever more complex hardware and software as time marches on are almost boundless. However with only a finite amount of pages available, I will point out some of what appears to be more noteworthy changes on the horizon that should be approached, considered and worked with:

Rise of Mobile Threats (ie Terrorists)- Terrorism, though gaining a considerable level of infamy in a post 9/11 era, has actually been around as far back as the 11th century by such groups as the Hashashins, or as they are better know them today, the Assassins.[51] They were a group that was well known for using unconventional tactics, psychological warfare and various terrorist measures to instill fear and terror in support of their political aspirations. In those times, terrorists had to rely almost completely on stealth, covert weaponry such as daggers and insider access or innovative ability to accomplish said tasks due the general lack of guns, explosives and other more convenient ways of assassinating different officials.

The modern day terrorist faces no such conundrum. One of the strengths of terror-based groups such as Al-Qaeda is their ability to blend in with their surroundings, and more importantly that

---

[51] Lewis, Bernard. *The Assassins: A Radical Sect in Islam*. London: Phoenix, 2003. Print.

they are attempting to capitalize on what the Information Age has to offer. They use the Internet to facilitate communications, social media to spread their message, CD's/DVD's and USB thumb drives to spread operational information, making use of publicly available encryption which is comparable to military strength encryption to protect their information from outside eyes and so forth.

The only boon to governments and militaries lately is the fact that what used to be considered one of the most deadly of terrorist groups, Al-Qaeda has somewhat faded into the background of the terror scene due to an over decade long struggle with the United States. Because of the extended engagement, not only has there been a considerable talent drain as their senior members are killed off but also much of their money has become focused on critical operations rather than on utilizing cyberwarfare. Because of this dearth of cash, most of Al-Qaeda's operational funding of technology has mostly leaned towards either extremely low cost or free software or hardware. However there is a storm brewing in the distance as other groups are becoming savvier to the benefits of low cost, low-tech cyberwar. Low cost

UAV's are starting to become more prevalent, websites promoting particular political causes are virtually effortless to create, DDoS attacks can be purchased from different groups who control botnets, not to mention that it takes little to no effort to begin digging up and cutting fiber optic cabling which in some cases provides the majority of Internet access for a given country. Other possible novel attack vectors include utilizing the so-called Raspberry Crazy Ant. In early 2013, there was computer and technology failures that were discovered to have been caused by these types of ants, who have seem to have an affinity for chewing on electrical wiring and insulation. Imagine the chagrin of a major computer and telecommunications agency at having major disruptions in their ability to conduct operations thanks to an insider with a bag full of electrical-wiring consuming ants! Ants of mass destruction, who'd have thought it?

Though these novel, and in some case typical attacks seem nerve-wracking at first glance however that should be attributed to the fact that they tend to be new or novel ideas rather than being truly fearsome weapons. Reasonable concern should be given towards the multitude of issues that we face in the future as the best answer is to patiently look the new innovations and adaptations as every new thing is looked upon: Consider the implications, make plans as appropriate and move on. It may be impossible to prepare and prevent every possible attack considering the endless ingenious ability for humans to innovate, (Simply look at the inside of any prison or correctional institute in the word to see the many incredible ways that weapons and tools are fashioned by men with nothing but time on their hands) however it takes little effort to consider the issue at hand and to at least prepare a contingency plan for it.

The advent of both modern technology along with quick adoption by terrorist groups followed by the slow adoption by governments and increasing public dependence on technology means that future terrorists will become more capable than ever of increasing their attack and communications capabilities through cyberwarfare. The trend should continue to be watched as governments either finds ways to more quickly adapt.

Rise of the Poor- At first glance, the title "Rise of the Poor" doesn't appear particularly alarming yet is a concept that could cause important shifts and accretion of power in unlikely countries that warrants a further look. The Internet is a global network that has connected us all, and slowly but surely countries which do not have as much technology as their much more rich counterparts are becoming connected, the free access of information can offer a surprising counter-effect if used properly.

In the beginning of this book we used the country classification system to help break down and define the different types of countries along with how well cyberwar could be reasonably be prosecuted against each country. Our concept of "Rise of the Poor" is related to countries that have been rated at the Level X classification level and will Future consideration should be given to countries which do not have much of a dependence on technology, such as perhaps Paraguay, and are able to become connected enough to the Internet that people began gaining much information for free. The Internet is a wellspring of free information, including on advanced computing, robotics, methods/development of offensive cyberwarfare, programming methods and so forth.

A country, such as of the "X" variety that have little dependence on technology vice say televisions or cell phones, but then begin rapidly developing a cyberwar capability to increase their standing in the world/strike at enemies could be much more dangerous in the realm of cyberwar. They have everything to gain through prosecution of technological warfare, with little infrastructure to be hit themselves. Giving the level X designation should be done with care of course as some countries which would seem to intuitively fall in such a category, such as North Korea, would not really fit as easily at first glance. The X designation assumes that the populace in general has connections to the Internet and a government that can harness the collective abilities of their people, find those who are skilled in particular parts of warfare, and begin developing capabilities. North Korea does to some extent have capability, however are excessively hobbled by their almost complete blackout of Internet communications and the desire to keep as many North Koreans off the Internet as possible. Because of this, there may be many talented people who could actually advance their countries cyberwar capacity considerable, but are never discovered.

This information shouldn't startle or raise fear of the poor or poor countries, but efforts should be instead made to strive and work diplomatically with the realization that someday, with the free spread of information, countries with the Level X designation could become a formidable adversary through this new type of warfare. (Not to mention simply sending people to other countries and having them conduct warfare through there so as the host country could deny their involvement completely.)

When all is said and done, the spread of free information shouldn't be viewed through a negative lens but rather based on the comparative benefits that will raise the stability of countries globally in contradiction to those who are unable to afford an expensive education. They will be able to learn more from the Internet for free than they otherwise would ever be able to learn otherwise do their impoverished status, thus offering far greater benefits then issues to be concerned about. However as always, erring on the side of caution and keeping an eye on future concerns remains a

Integration of Cloud Based Hacking- We are currently seeing a seismic shift from traditional server based computing in many corporations to what is known as "Cloud based" services. Using Cloud services has been a boon for many a company, allowing them to shift the burden off of themselves to maintain expensive servers and associated costs. "Cloud Services" are essentially a service offered by major organizations such as Amazon or Salesforce which allow a business to take advantage of the gigantic server farms they host to run applications. It greatly reduces, if not eliminates the need for servers and substantially increases cost savings for the business involved. Another type of cloud service (Similar to grid computing software that was especially prevalent in the early 2000's.) is that which allows people to harness the larger clusters of CPU/GPU cycles of these companies to run complex operations that could typically require significantly more finance on a supercomputer.

Though still in its infancy for all intents and purposes, the staggering technological capability that this offers to individual actors, groups and even countries is substantial in terms of instant strength, virtually anywhere in the world. Cloud services can be used for attempting to brute force passwords to encrypted files, for breaking system administrator passwords, storing encrypted files for intelligence services, storing electronic money anonymously to be moved around the world and in particular, offering support for espionage operations.

The ability to bring the entire power of cloud servers to bear anywhere in the world, at virtually anytime is something we should keep an eye on. (In particular once cloud servers begin to use any quantum technology that comes around in the future.)

Miniaturization/Virtual Hacking systems- As we were previously discussing, the world of technology is advancing at a breakneck pace. CPU's continue to become exponentially more powerful, storage drives continue to explode in terms of space, however we should also note the power of increasing miniaturized computers, such as the Raspberry Pi. This tiny system, currently available for the incredibly cheap price of $49, is roughly the size of a small cookie and is a full size computer with a network connector, USB connector, monitor connection and so forth. This will represent a huge field in which should be study just as intensely as the others. These tiny, yet decently powered computers can be used for any number of tasks: For example, acting as the computing base for drones in countries that cannot afford traditional drone technology, for espionage purposes such as plugging a Pi into a system which then automatically runs scripts to hack the system/provide access to outsiders, and so forth.

Of further mention would be the previously mentioned miniaturized satellites called Cubesats. These relatively inexpensive, miniaturized satellites that can be launched by the average person and provide basic capabilities, such as audio playback, transmission upload/downloads and so forth. The ability for anyone in the world to launch a low-cost satellite into space would offer a previously unheard of opportunity for any country, or even militaries/espionage groups to begin starting small scale space programs to support both logistics and allow capabilities which were previously financially infeasible.

One example of such a capability would be a person stealing classified information, loading it remotely into a Cubesat floating in space and having it broadcast to the agent's home country via encrypted satellite transmission. The innovative possibilities for adaptation to cyberwarfare are practically limitless.

The Surveillance State- Surveillance has long been the hallmark of governments the military towards aiding operations at large. It allows the surreptitious collection of information and to properly prepare for the future, however with the current level of technology in the world, surveillance has moved up to a level never before conceived. GPS trackers can be placed on vehicles to monitor their every movement, spy satellites can be used to literally count the hairs on a person head, companies such as Google keep records of every web search a person makes through its search engine, while even phone companies have become complicit in tracking, which was particularly revealed through the discovery of the FBI's use of the

"Stingray" program, which involved faking cellular towers along with vacuuming up mass amounts of information.

There are two considerations regarding the future "Surveillance State":

1) How do we conduct surveillance more effectively because of future technology?
2) How can we more effectively /defeat/ future surveillance technology.

It appears that just as with terrorism, innovative ability tends to trump billions of dollars in advanced technology. Drones were used for a long time to track terrorists in Afghanistan in Iraq, then it was discovered that insurgents were hacking their unencrypted video feeds. GPS signals can be scrambled. People can use encrypted VOIP voice circuits rather than speaking over traditional cellular connections, and so forth.

To more effectively perform surveillance, it appears that two considerations are paramount:

1) Focus on low-cost innovation: There are indeed some ideas that are worth pouring billions of dollars into for defeating low-cost ideas, however the emphasis should be on low-cost ideas that do nearly or as good a job as the more expensive idea. The rationale behind this is obvious, as once the hi-tech/expensive solution is discovered, then the financially deficient, yet an innovative enemy will come up with yet another cunning defeater for it. Innovative talent must be retained. Rather than focusing financial resources on technology, it instead should be used to harvest top notch talent that will continue coming up with future disruptive ideas.

2) Except for game changers, avoid expensive technology: Such as with Atlas, and drone technology, the money is well spent and does effectively change the face of warfare itself and how it is prosecuted. However there are a multitude of bad ideas which are not as well thought out. As previously said, the money should be aimed squarely at attracting the brightest talent who show an aptitude for

innovation. (Not solely because of a college degree or two hanging on their wall.)

To attempt to more effectively combat technical surveillance, two considerations are important to consider:

1) In general, it is assumed that if one is attempting to combat targeted technical surveillance that they are at a considerable disadvantage.
2) Assume that virtually all communication devices and electronics can be manipulated to record video or audio without a person's knowledge or permission.

Internet Killswitches- Proposals have been floating in some countries, including the United States for a "killswitch" for the Internet. The scope varies, however this is a contingency that one would have to plan for if possible. There have been examples of such a killswitch used in the past, such as in Syria, when the Internet was completely cut off from the outside for periods of time. However they only cut off the Internet from within their borders, plus the Internet Service

Providers were likely closely affiliated/overrun by the state government. In other countries where there is a considerable diversity of Internet providers, this would likely prove more difficult to unilaterally accomplish.

However, the creator of these killswitches appears to be displaying a fundamental misunderstanding of the Internet: The Internet was created to be one of the most redundant, self-healing network circuits ever conceived in history. Even if over half of the Internet was shutdown, the switches and backbones that keep it up would simply reconfigure their network pathways to adapt and keep the Internet up. In cases such as Syria, people were able to be reconnected via foreign nationals who infiltrated into the country and setup mobile cellular/Internet connection towers, satellite connections would remain intact, people can dial out to Internet service providers outside of the country through traditional telephone landlines and through other innovative ways of connection that have not yet been conceived.

In short: Internet kill switches should be considered cautiously before creating, and particularly before deploying. When such a system is being considered to be put in place, it shows that the government fears the people, regardless of what ruse they attempt to disguise the rationale behind. (Terrorists, hackers, etc.) However if such a system is created regardless and deployed, it should further be noted that deploying such a system is akin to marital law and in some countries, would actually have a virtually paralyzing effect. (Imagine when for example, entire stock market exchanges are shut down to the inability for investors to access their funds!)

The Rise of Digital Currency- Though a more recent design, digital currency has exploded on the scene in a way that no one could have foreseen. Unlike traditional currency, such as dollars or yuan, digital currency is a new medium of buying and selling which uses cryptographic-based currency generated through the competition of complex mathematical problems. One of the leading digital currencies that currently exist is Bitcoin, which despite wild volatility in price is currently valued at $920 a coin as of this writing. Essentially one can either generate bitcoins through computer based mining activity or through buying bitcoins at various exchanges.

Many governments are still examining the future role of cryptographic-based currency, with some having given a relatively neutral reaction such as the United States to others which have been outright hostile (China) to actually raiding the exchanges themselves. (India) However there appears to be somewhat an ignorance to the staggering game changer that this currency remains to be. The possibilities for moving money at lightning speeds with little to no oversight via innovative ways is almost limitless.

Suppose you wanted to move $100,000 from Spain to the United States. Attempting to do so via traditional means such as through airplane luggage can be quite difficult. Airlines check luggage often, so attempting to move that size of money without declaring it would not only risk forfeiture of it all, but also some possibly serious questions from customs agents along with possible deportation. Moving from banks would also be a concern, because for the most part, banks appear to play by the rules in regards to transferring money between countries because of fear of running afoul of anti-terror regulations. Generally, banks can be expected to report large transfers of currency inside of their respective countries and particularly between countries. However cryptocurrency such as Bitcoin completely changes all of that. It is a trifle matter to buy bitcoins from say a Japanese based exchange, such as MtGox or one of the many other exchanges in the world, move to another country and then withdraw the money in the local currency. Of course there are attempts to legitimize such money as exchanges attempt to voluntarily follow anti-money laundering laws, but it remains to see how effective they will truly be in the long run due the fact that by and large, bitcoin is completely anonymous. (Some disagree, regarding anonymity as possible to track through transactions to some extent via the bitcoin blockchain, however with the advent of "tumbler" sites and software they are effectively anonymous vice a considerable effort made by governments to track a particular transaction. One that would take far too long to likely catch the perpetrator.)

As previously stated, the possibilities are limitless. For example, if an intelligence agency desired to move money to finance operations in a hostile foreign environment, it would be simple to transfer bitcoin from one online wallet to another online wallet. The bitcoins could then be withdrawn in local currency. (There would be no more moving hundreds of thousands of dollars in suitcases to support remote operations: You could literally move millions in mere seconds with just a few keystrokes on a laptop or taps on a smartphone.)

Beyond the ability to move money for criminal organizations, intelligence agencies and the military, there is also considerable opportunity for government organizations and financial institutions. Governments could make untraceable payoffs to other countries, politicians could receive and pay off bribery money without much fear of a money trail. Financial institutions could possibly attempt to manipulate currency through massive shifts of one currency into bitcoin, then transfer it to another country so as to devalue it. Even worse, terrorist organizations could make massive transfers of wealthy with a reduced fear of discovery by anti-laundering organizations and governments.

Though the future of digital currency is foggy due the fact that it still remains in its infancy as we speak, however I suspect that what will likely take place will be governments who are smart to the advantages and implications of bitcoin will quietly create their own government backed version of digital currency, shut down bitcoin through legislation and use it to alter the world of finance and business transactions in a way never before seen or could have ever been anticipated. Even the revolution engendered by credit cards will likely pale in comparison, however suppressing fear future software and remaining fluid with change is the key to the future. Jump on the train and analyze how to harness it for future use rather than simply attempting to stomp innovation for outdated methods.

Rise of Cyberwarfare: Throughout this book we have explored the different avenues and effects that attacking through technology can have. The crux of the damage that can be inflicted tends to be directly proportional to the level of dependence that the population has on technology itself. (Which of course can include any type of technology, such as radios, TV's, cars and so forth.) The exponential growth and spread of technology over the last decade has been breathtaking however it is quickly becoming apparent that we are only on the cusp of this revolution. Faster, more powerful technology is being created year by year while the world becomes further integrated into the global grid and people become more dependent on said technology than ever before.

Multiple game changing technologies are already around the corner, such as quantum computing and cryptography, which will almost immediately make all current computers and encryption standards obsolete. Changes in the amount of storage space available for computers are also exploding from a theoretical standpoint. At the moment, the average external hard drive can contain up to 1-4 terabytes of information whereas there is a new storage disk available called the "Quartz Disk" which can hold up to 360 terabytes of information. Often, technology that was previously considered science fiction tends to spark the imagination of people growing up, and often this idea tends to become reality.

However despite what is now the new front of warfare that is emerging, the attention that appears to be given to it is scant as compared to other disciplines. Media outlets are filled with embarrassing coverage that appears more to scare rather than inform the public, many governments are content to only pay lip service in finance and talent towards their militaries in cyberwar while many could care less about it as there has not yet been a catastrophic attack involving cyberwar. Yet, that is. While considering different aspects of history, usually it appears that a major terrifying attack is what precipitates a military or other defense organizations getting the funding they need to defend against such a threat. This was particularly expressed in the case of the September 11th attacks in 2001 on the United States by Al-Qaeda. Chronic underfunding had caused problems both in the US Military and the Central Intelligence Agency, however after post 9/11 there was such a sudden surge in funding for intelligence operations and special operations units that it was considered virtually out of control.

When all is said and done, it is my greatest hope that those who read this book will consider the necessity for preparing at least minimally for cyberwarfare instead of waiting for the first technological Pearl Harbor to hit instead.

Chapter 10: Closing Thoughts

Some years ago when I was serving on active in the Navy at a NATO base in Spain, a curious event took place. At the time, I was working as lead Helpdesk technician and had arrived to get started on another typical day in the office. While starting the morning up conversing with bleary eyed co-workers, I mentioned some of the surprising advancements in technology that only 5-10 years prior were generally considered almost impossible, such as the military fielding weapons grade laser technology. (Though there were ambitious programs that attempted to make such dreams come true, such as former US president Ronald Reagans Strategic Defense initiative in the early 1980's which were widely derided as impossible.) One of my Army co-workers at the time laughed incredulously, saying something along the lines of my "..need to get my head out of the clouds."[52] Needless to say I was the one that was shocked, as chemical-based lasers had already been available for some time in the US Air Force aboard planes and was being tested for possible use in overloading the optic guidance systems of missiles.

---

[52] This quote is paraphrased. Those of us in the military tend to use a bit more colorful language.

(After providing a recent copy of the Air Force Times publication the laughter faded.)

However I do not believe the ignorance of that mentality is confined to one person alone, but instead is indicative of general disinterest towards in technology that does not directly affect the person themselves. This is further exacerbated by the breakneck pace at which the world is changing and moving forward. People fear that which they do not understand while many have neither the time nor the inclination to learn about every new gadget as much as we do not have the time to learn everything about our car; we instead bring it to a mechanic.

Now how can we go about reversing this trend and work towards getting more interest in fields related to cyberwar? The answer lies simply in how we perceive people and the ways they conduct their lives.

Often it is the case that when the average person applies for a job, they will submit their resumes, are screened through pre-written algorithms in computer systems for the usual checkmarks (College degree, previous experience and favorable words from prior employers among other achievements) and then likely passed over. However there is a notable lack by both Research and Development sections of major corporations and government research facilities to consider the intangible portions which can make a candidate better than another. Certainly there are candidates with experience and education that seem to make them stand out however there are no apparent markers or interviews that tests or determines the breadth of ability in intuition, innovative thinking, quick thinking and other traits. There are likely many in the public, simply living their lives without any realization of the latent innovative ability they possess and are waiting to be picked up by a research think tank that will allow them to think outside the box. The beauty of innovation is that it doesn't require someone with a Ph.D in Computer Science, or 20 years of engineering experience at a major corporation. Truth be told, there are many more people with higher level graduate education and experience then there are true innovators who can only have little more than a cursory understanding of specific equipment, yet be able to utilize in a way never considered.

Education and experience should not be discounted of course, and are both not only important but also are more likely to bring something to the table than those with lesser education or experience. However governments in particular should be more proactive in how they seek out talent rather than simple posting on Monster.com or putting out the occasional job ad. A full court press should be made towards aggressively seeking out talent that can provide outside the box ideas which are potential game changers. For example seeking out those with education that tends to lean more towards the abstract, such as in the liberal arts, or looking into industries where creativity is the norm. People with little to no engineering experience may not know the intricacies of the equipment they are looking at, however there is no shortage of ways in which to implement such things when the basics are understood.

Even more worrying than the potential waste of talent is the fact that there are people who do possess considerable talent at both innovation and computing however perhaps lack the credentials or industry experience to pass through the hoops necessary to get into typical computer security jobs. Some are simply passed by because of their lack of people skills which despite being a necessary trait, should instead be looked out within the proper context: Are corporations or government agencies really willing to pass up on the next potential Einstein simply because of a lack of cultural sense or struggles to get along with others? The though is simply unconscionable.

A large portion of this book has been written regarding the necessity for innovation because it remains one of the most important parts of such warfare. Technology and computers in particular are evolving and growing at such a rapid pace that the necessity for finding and incubating the talent that can handle such a pace is becoming critical. Governments and corporations need to seek not only smart, but innovative minds that do not necessarily hold the typical degrees from prestigious institutions.

In addition to keeping an eye out for educated people, there is an additional human trait that continually contends for the same level of importance which is a person who has their finger on the pulse of where the newest technology is at and where it is going. There has to be a passion for technology which progresses beyond a simple desire to complete the end of a work day but rather instead strive forward for love of the game, learning something new and being on the cutting edge of a field that is both different and exciting. This goes hand in hand with the desire to innovate and hack new technology to make it do things that were not originally intended, and will prove to be the mentality and mind behind great cybersoldiers of the future.

www.ingramcontent.com/pod-product-compliance
Lightning Source LLC
Chambersburg PA
CBHW051049050326
40690CB00006B/660